The Declaration of Global Civilization

The Declaration of Global Civilization

SHAOHUA ZHANG
Chairman of OPGC
Translated by Vincent Law

iUniverse, Inc.
New York Lincoln Shanghai

The Declaration of Global Civilization

iUniverse books may be ordered through booksellers or by contacting:

iUniverse
2021 Pine Lake Road, Suite 100
Lincoln, NE 68512
www.iuniverse.com
1-800-Authors (1-800-288-4677)

The views expressed herein are the sole responsibility of the author and do not necessarily reflect the views of iUniverse or its affiliates.

ISBN-13: 978-0-595-41264-8 (pbk)
ISBN-13: 978-0-595-85619-0 (cloth)
ISBN-13: 978-0-595-85618-3 (ebk)
ISBN-10: 0-595-41264-5 (pbk)
ISBN-10: 0-595-85619-5 (cloth)
ISBN-10: 0-595-85618-7 (ebk)

Printed in the United States of America

- The Declaration on Global Civilization is a most impressive document providing a blueprint for approaching the increasingly urgent problems facing humanity. Comprehensive and subtle, it weaves into a firm but tolerant synthesis the best elements of past and present world civilizations. All would benefit from reflecting on the Declaration's analysis and proposals which embody the best response to the crisis of our times.

  David McLellan
  Professor of Political Theory
  University of London, UK

- The Declaration provides a vision of a brighter future for all human beings on earth.

  William O. Beeman
  Professor of Anthropology
  Brown University, USA

- The Declaration has laid out a theoretical foundation for human society in the twenty-first century to progress towards world peace. It provides solutions to resolve conflicts between nations, cultures, and religions in the global world. The most needed catalyst to uplift humanity.

  Yuri V. Yakovets
  Professor
  Russian Academy of Public Administration Under President of Russian Federation

- The concept in the Declaration is a seed for new humankind and new civilization that is capable of resolving current global problems. It is an initiate conception, and from this point, the future of humankind is wide-open.

  Qinghai Gao
  Professor of Philosophy
  Jilin University, China

- The concepts elucidated in this Declaration are extremely interesting and of great importance to the whole of humanity. It illuminates a serious situation facing all of humanity, insofar as we share one planet and one world. It theorizes on how we got to this point and suggests how we, as citizens of a global civilization, need to realign our thinking in order to survive the impending chaos.

    Editorial Evaluation
    iUniverse Inc.

CONTENTS

The Declaration of Global Civilization[1]

Initiated and organized by the Organization for Promoting Global Civilization (OPGC), the First World Congress of Global Civilization was held at the Hilton Hotel in Sydney, Australia, from July 16 to July 18, 2001. Fifty representatives and 30 invited guests from 37 countries from science, religious, politic, literary, art, and business circles were in attendance. This Declaration of Global Civilization was passed and adopted in the Congress by a vote of 46 to1, with two participants abstaining, and one not participating. This declaration is about the destiny of humanity. **It is the first theoretical declaration in history that is written for all human societies.**

I. Overview and Discussion

This year, the year 2001, is the first year of the new century and the new millennium. Human evolution is now entering into a crucial transition period that has significance equal to the time when humanity was developed from the animal kingdom. There are two signs forecasting the dawn of this transitional period: first, the focal point of human progress is moving away from traditional focuses throughout history, such as the mode of production, social systems, and ideologies and towards the domain of Civilization—the core of human existence. Second, human society is becoming a Global World—the broadest sphere of

---

1   The first draft of this declaration was discussed from July to December 1999 by a group of scholars from the United States, Russia, China, the United Kingdom, India, Iran, Singapore, Romania, Australia, New Zealand, and other states. The second draft was circulated worldwide from January to December 2000, to solicit comments. It attracted overwhelming attention, support, and comments from people from 97 countries, including heads of state, religious leaders, and Nobel Prize laureates. The third draft was submitted for discussion and debate in the First World Congress of Global Civilization and was passed and adopted in that Congress. The first draft, the second draft, the version for discussion used in the First Congress, and this current version are written and revised by Mr. Shaohua Zhang, a Chinese scholar and the Chairman of the Organization for Promoting Global Civilization. The Chinese version is the original and standard version of this declaration. This English version was translated by Vincent Law.

human activity—instead of the traditional tribal world, national world, or international world.

The issue of Civilization is to be the dominant force in the twenty-first century. In the century of civilization, only a civilization-based solution can truly resolve the most pressing global issues. In the century of globalization, only a Global Civilization can fundamentally change the destiny of humanity for the better.

We should not be satisfied in merely realizing that we are in a century of civilization—it is already an unquestionable fact. We should not indulge in talking the talks about promoting a World Civilization, an Earth Civilization, or a Human Civilization—it will make no difference to the real world. We should not expect a magic formula to free us from civilizational conflicts—it will only lead to the contrary.

Today, it is fundamentally crucial to let people know what kind of civilization we really need in the global age. It is profoundly important to let people know that the real origin of civilization conflicts lies within civilization itself. That is, a theoretical preparation is a must before we can find practical solutions to unavoidable civilization-based conflict in the global world. The purpose of writing, discussing, and adopting this declaration is to have a thorough theoretical anatomy of Civilization. It attempts to end the prolonged history of promoting civilization by uncivilized means, hence to lead humankind to a world of peace and harmony.

1   The Initiation and Purpose of Global Civilization

The second half of the twentieth century was a period of unprecedented global chaos caused by civilization-based conflicts. In most regions and states, the backbone of civilization—law, order, and faith—had come to the edge of collapse; the inner vitality of civilization—trust, belief, and self-confidence—had been drastically decaying. The level of family ethics, social morals, government functions, and ideology had been sharply declining. On the other hand, the rate of crime, drug trafficking, terrorist acts, and cultural/religious violence has been steadily climbing. Reconfiguration of global politics, military alliances, and nuclear weapons deployment based on cultural affinity is becoming an open act rather than a condemned secret. Powerful, large nations, and core states of civilization are no exception. In the meantime, the public sentiments of ethnocentrism, nationalism, patriotism, together with antipatriotism, anarchism, and antigovernmentalism that all originated from a strong desire to maintain cultural identity in the global world, are particularly evident among young students and intellectual elites. A deluge of these sentiments has overrun people's common sense and drowned human conscience.

In short, "He who serves God for money is serving the devil for better wages," is still a worldwide reality today. Humanity is giving way to extreme egotism and the law of the jungle. In the beginning of this new millennium, such sinister developments in the international political arena are a stark reminder of the violent conflicts of the last century. Humankind is on the verge of repeating a tragic history. People are expressing a great concern: "a global Dark Age, [is] possibly descending on humanity."[2]

It is absolutely necessary to have a thorough analysis of the cause of this global chaos. The two consecutive world wars in the first half of the twentieth century took all nations onto the global political stage. The devastating wars consequently produced a period of peacetime—a period, ironically, we call the Cold War. The aftermath of war was a very favorable environment for technological development with military upgrading as its incentive. Modernization of technology created economic globalization, and globalization, in turn, stimulated scientific and technological development. On the superficial level, the pervasive political and military competition between the Western Bloc, the Eastern Bloc, and the Third World community, together with the mutual catalytic forces of globalization and modernization, has disguised the underlying cultural conflict. In fact, all nations in the wave of globalization and modernization have brought their own cultures and beliefs into one confrontational arena at a modern speed. In a time of increasing globalization and modernization, the deeply rooted self-consistency of each civilization and the instinctive desire to maintain cultural identity will eventually lead to dangerous clashes. Some might even be large-scale collective battles.

After Word War II, a common answer to the challenge of increasing interaction and confrontation between different cultures and beliefs was "returning to the roots." From remote rural areas to sophisticated urban societies, from young students to academic elites, from general public to state leaders, every nation, every culture, every religion, every individual was asking the same questions with great enthusiasm. "Who are we?" "Who are our ancestors?" "Who are they?" "Where are they leading us to?" Searching for answers to these questions led to the establishment of some transnational confederations based on cultural affinity, such as the European Union, the Arab League, and the African League. It also led to the quick end of a century-long colonial era and the rapid disintegration of other forms of transcivilizational alliances, including the short-lived Eastern Bloc.

---

2   Huntington, S. P. (1996): *The Clash of Civilizations and the Remaking of World Order*. Simon & Schuster: New York. Page 321. Chapter 12. The West, Civilizations, and Civilization.

The collapse of the Eastern bloc and the disintegration of the Warsaw Pact left the Western allies without rivals. The United States, as the only superpower in the world, took the lead in a rapid Western expansion. Western civilization, especially American values and beliefs, through its technological advantage, economic strength, and military might, awakened all other civilizations in the world from prolonged dormancy. Without preparation, non-Western societies reacted to the Western impact and came to the battlefield hostile. This scenario of ugly encounters, in turn, was beyond Western anticipation. Thus in the collective battlefield of civilization, no one was prepared, and no judge was on duty. Every party involved was full of self-esteem but lacked self-confidence. We can clearly see that in this civilization chaos, all parties have much in common: they all tried to resolve cultural/religious conflicts in a new global world by traditional means—through outmoded colonial thinking, hegemonic mentality, and hopeless addiction to the use of force; they all tried to participate in globalization and modernization from the perspective of their own interests, traditions and cultures. In other words, while all nations are enthusiastically embracing globalization and modernization, they were desperately defending their indigenous values and beliefs.

Apparently, this is a period of globalization and modernization without theoretical, political, and psychological preparedness. It is a time of cultural convergence entered into with passiveness, blindness, and extemporaneousness. This has inevitably created a rather absurd phenomenon—the global integration and modern interaction has turned the long passed ancient hatred between nations, the reasonable difference between states, and the historical limitation in cultures into non-civilized relationships ruled by self-centered nationalism, ethnocentrism, religious conceit, and cultural discrimination.

Uncivilized interaction inevitably leads to an anti-civilization outcome. Each nation is determined to defend its culture, even if the price it pays is a violation of the fundamental principles of humanity—the essence of civilization from thousands of years of human quest. Although they are part of the modernization and globalization physically, they are retreating from a global society and modern civilization morally. It is not an overstatement to say that in most cases every civilization reacted to cultural conflicts by insanely intensifying its unhealthy aspects and senselessly infringing its positive merits. This, in turn, stimulated the negative aspects of its rivals and shrunk the healthy aspects of other civilizations. Unfortunately, these positive merits that were abandoned were the golden harvest of civilization that each nation had been cultivating throughout generations—a universal spirit of civilization with eternality. This can be clearly exemplified by major international events after World War II, such as the arms race between the United States and the Soviet Union during the Cold War, the Korean War, the Vietnam War, the Soviet invasion of Afghanistan, the Iran-Iraq War, the Iraqi invasion of Kuwait, the Gulf War, the NATO eastward expansion, as well as numerous conflicts within sovereign states, such as the Rwanda genocide, the ethnic cleansing against Kurds in Iraq, the Srebrenica massacre, the Chinese Cultural Revolution, and the tragic acts of the Taliban regime in Afghanistan to name a few. What concerns people most is that such tragedies may just be the beginning of a chaotic time.[3]

What causes this and who is to blame? It may be argued that it is nobody's fault. There was always a very "good" reason behind every warfare and tragedy. Each reason could be perfectly justified within a narrow cultural context. So shall we blame the law of evolution and the time if it is nobody's fault? In fact, the law of evolution and the time are two Angels who are selflessly guiding human progress without ever making a mistake. Humankind is in the quest of this truth: increasing globalization has caused a global chaos that is generating strong discontentment and painful reflection on the limitedness, one-sidedness, obsoleteness, and extremeness of all civilizations. The discontentment and reflection are now preparing humanity for a different civilization—the darkness of the global chaos

---

3   Further analysis is needed here. Economic globalization is caused by the modernization of science and technology. Western civilization is the driving force of modernization. However, globalization is not colonization and modernization does not mean Westernization because economic activity and scientific/technologic development are only the outer form of civilization at the surface layer, whereas cultural value and custom are the middle layer, and realization of humanity and enriching individuality are at the core. It is possible for a stronger state to occupy a smaller country and rule its people, but it is far more difficult to control their beliefs and souls. With the marketplace globalized and technology spread worldwide, American-led Western civilization is bringing its values to all non-Western civilizations. Although this fits into the common logic of civilizational evolution, it inevitably triggers strong resistance from non-Western societies and causes a large-scale civilizational warfare at a deeper level. Confronting this situation, non-Western civilizations are forced to rethink their cultural identity. This, in turn, forces Western civilization to do the same.

In the second half of the twentieth century, particularly its last two decades, every nation was looking for a protective shell of civilization to deal with the sudden flooding of globalization and modernization. Although the West creates globalization and modernization, the West does not have the privilege of exclusive ownership. In fact, globalization and modernization is the inevitable result of human progress and should be used to benefit the whole human race. That is to say, globalization is a trend that cannot be stopped and should not be detoured or turned backward. If so, the shell of local/regional civilizations in this warfare, although effective for thousands of years, is no longer a safe hideout for non-Western societies. More significantly, the striking contrast and violent clashing between globalization and local civilization, between modernization and tradition, is causing internal turmoil and in-depth distortion for every non-Western society.

of civilization-based conflicts is, in fact, indicating that humanity is about to see the dawn of a new civilization characterized by Global Civilization.

People are shaped by their civilization and are shaping their civilization in turn. Most importantly, people are the driving force of a new civilization. Confronting the possibility of regional war, world war, genocide, and religious violence caused by civilization clashes, humankind has no choice but to thoroughly investigate all existing civilizations, expose their harmful element and outmoded thinking that starts conflicts and clashes.

Looking around the world today, we can find encouraging evidence that underneath the surface of a global chaos, a hope of humanity and the spirit of a global civilization is quietly emerging in many countries in various ways: Australian multiculturalism promotes harmony among different cultures; the Singaporean way integrates Western and Eastern values; the American spirit values human rights as its fundamental principle; the Iranian Civilization Dialogue proactively opens its door to the world for better understanding; the revival of Taoism-Confucianism in China emphasizes the unity of the world and the law of nature; Russian new thinking repositions itself in international politics; and the UN resolution names the first year of the new millennium as the year of civilization dialogue, to name but a few. Although these attempts may be experimental, the underlying tendency is evident: they all try to overcome the parochialism of local civilization. Each attempt is one step closer towards global civilization.

If this is correct, then those prevailing theories, such as the Clash of Civilizations, Cultural Indigenization, and Return to The Roots, although based on current reality, are directing people in a regressive way. Some contrasting approaches, such as Civilization Dialogue, Cultural Pluralism, and Cultural Assimilation, although expressing the goodwill of today's people, are short in objective foundation. It is neither possible to truly resolve the deep-seated cultural conflict, nor is it possible to have a real dialogue among civilizations because, within the current framework of sovereign state, within a parochial circle of local culture, under the predominate thinking of current civilizations, the mindset of state primacy, the idea of self-centered culture, and the sentiment of religious fundamentalism, are the exact origins of civilization clash and the obstacles to dialogue among civilizations. This is because any civilization is proficient in managing its internal issues but it was never designed to resolve problems between civilizations. Trans-civilizational conflict can only be resolved by a trans-civilizational way, a way that manifests the essence of all local civilizations but at a higher level. Global Civilization is the way.[4]

---

4   For example, following the turmoil and chaos at the end of twentieth century, most politicians, religious leaders, scholars, and the general public from every corner of the world were calling for remaking a new world political and economic order. To make a world order applicable to the majority of the world, it is absolutely necessary to nurture a spirit of a universal civilization—the spirit of Global Civilization.

In short, the common origin for the 5000-year-old local civilization model, for the 300-year-old civilization expansion momentum, and for the 50 years of overwhelming violence, warfare, and ugly cultural/religious conflicts after World War II is an absence of a transnational, transregional spirit, a spirit of a universal civilization—the Spirit of Global Civilization. History is now pointing twenty-first-century humankind to the last and the only pathway towards a brighter future: **globalization and modernization within the parameter of a common humanity and the collective welfare extracting the beneficial element from all civilizations and cultivating them into a new universal and modern civilization that transcends local civilizations—Global Civilization.**[5]

Clearly, only in the light of Global Civilization can the commonality of different civilizations become apparent. Only then can the exposure of both the beneficial and the harmful elements of each civilization become possible. Only then can we find the safe interacting platform for civilizations and the right path to elevate local civilizations. This is the essential purpose of Global Civilization.

2   The Definition and Principle of Global Civilization

Civilization can be defined in a broad sense and in a narrow sense. In its narrow sense, civilization is contrasted with ignorance, barbarism, and primitivism. This is also its absolute meaning. In a broader sense, civilization refers to the mode of human existence and its development. As a mode of existence, it could be civilized at one time but uncivilized in another, so has a relative meaning underlying.

Before the global age, civilization normally referred to the common mode of existence within the complexity of distinct societies. Thus all civilizations that have occurred in history so far, including indigenous civilizations (such as tribes, nations, sovereign states) and regional civilizations (such as Europeans, Africans, Easterners, Westerners) are essentially Territorial Civilizations. Territorial Civilization is self-contained and civilized, but partial and exclusive. It has a strong instinct to reject, demolish, or fuse other civilizations, thus showing the non-civilized and anti-

---

5   We use the term Global Civilization instead of Human Civilization because the latter is not specific enough in this context. For example, any civilization, current or ancient, alive or dead, can be termed as human civilization. In contrast, Global Civilization is distinct from any model of existing civilization. It is a reflection of human aspiration to understand and advance civilization collectively. We do not use the term World Civilization because the definition of world is rather ambiguous, in history and in present times. World Civilization could not convey the true meaning of Global Civilization, whereas Global Civilization covers all implications in a deeper level that World Civilization intends to express.

civilized defects. This is the common characteristic and fatal flaw of all Territorial Civilizations.

In contrast, the explicit objective of Global Civilization is to promote all civilizations in the world. It reveals a universal civilization shared by every community of human society. Generally speaking, Global Civilization includes two meanings. First, it is a civilization of the global world. It inspires and helps each civilization to find the right path in the global world and elevate it into a higher level. This general definition emphasizes the individuality of every civilization. Second, it is a civilization with a global nature. That is to say, it is a universal civilization model that manifests a modern spirit. This specific definition emphasizes the commonality of all civilizations.[6] Promoting the civilization of the global world is the goal, and using the means of civilization with a global nature is the pathway towards this goal. These two meanings are mutually interconnected, supportive, and unified. Only with this goal and in this way can the human endeavor of promoting civilization by civilized means be possible.

More specifically, the meaning of Global Civilization has the following three aspects.

First, looking at its structure, Global Civilization is the unity of Human Civilization and Race Civilization. Generally speaking, the human race is the unity of humans and race. In this sense, Global Civilization is both an independent concept and a whole concept.

As an independent concept, it is defined using biological and anthropological perspectives with an emphasis on the species' existence of humanity. The significance lies in that only armed with the concept of Human Civilization—the idea that all peoples are human—can we discover the commonality among civilizations.

As a whole concept, it is defined using sociological perspectives and cultural theories with an emphasis on humanity being a collective whole integrated by individuals and societies. The significance lies in that only armed with the concept of Race Civilization—the principle that humankind is an organic whole (the

---

6   This means that Global Civilization does not exclude local civilizations. On the contrary, it is a rational response to the call to respect and protect indigenous civilization. More importantly, Global Civilization transcends all local civilizations that gives it such power—only the civilization with this global nature can provide direction of the modern society, provide solution to resolve civilization-based conflicts, provide the last and the strongest safeguard to avoid possible civilization-based warfare, from higher perspective and collective perspective.

idea that humankind has both biological naturality/Human Nature, and social morality/Race Nature)—can we be able to elevate local civilizations.[7]

With "all humans share one ancestor" being laid as one base and "humankind is one unity" being set as the other, the foundation of Global Civilization has been firmly grounded.

Second, looking at its content, Global Civilization is the unity of Individual Civilization and Collective Civilization. Strictly speaking, humanity is the unity of all individuals and the collective human race. In this sense, Global Civilization is both an elementary concept and a collective concept.

As an elementary concept, it is defined from an individual perspective. The significance of this lies in that only armed with the principle of Human Rights Civilization—the concept of a true civilization being a civilization deeply rooted in every individual—can we be able to determine beneficial or harmful elements in civilizations.

As a collective concept, it is defined from collective perspective. The significance of this lies in that only armed with the principle of Race Right Civilization—the concept of a true civilization being a civilization for the whole human race—can we be able to evaluate the level of civilization.[8]

---

[7] Human Civilization and Race Civilization form a unity. Any civilization that does not respect Human Nature (such as material needs, physical needs, and natural environment) should not be regarded as a "good" civilization. Conversely, any civilization that indulges in Human Nature but ignores Race Nature (such as social, cultural, and emotional needs) should not be regarded as a "good" civilization. Similarly, any civilization that does not respect properties defined by Human Nature (such as equality, freedom, and human rights) should not be regarded as a "good" civilization. Conversely, any civilization that indulges in properties defined by Human Nature but ignores properties defined by Race Nature (such as social responsibility, morality, and spiritual well-being) should not be regarded as a "good" civilization.

[8] Individual Civilization and Collective Civilization form an inherent unity. Fundamental individual needs are certainly collective needs. Things beneficial for the whole humanity are certainly beneficial for individuals. The direction of individual development always points to the collective whole. The direction of collective evolution always points to individuals. This is the secret of humanity and individuals. It is also the secret of any culture and civilization. From this standpoint, the human evolution is no more than the unity of two processes, namely individual development towards collective consciousness, and the collective development towards individual quality. Any civilization in history, including clan, tribe, chiefdom, state, and regional civilization, simply works as the transition and intermediary for these two processes during the whole span of human evolution.

Guiding individuals into a collective consciousness with one hand and translating collective faculty into individual quality with the other is the purpose of Global Civilization.

Third, looking at its defining features, Global Civilization is the unity of Prime Civilization and Greater Civilization. Holistically speaking, humankind is the unity of human existence and its environment. In this sense, Global Civilization is both a definite concept and an indefinite concept.

As a definite concept, it is defined from the perspective of human life existence. Civilization is a complete system of human existence that can be divided into three layers: the political, economic, and social structure is at the surface layer; custom, value, and faith make up the middle layer; the understanding and the quest of humanity, including its Human Nature, Race Nature, and collective/individualistic features, are the core layer. Any civilization is an organic whole of the social order, culture, and human consciousness. When we classify civilization as regional or national, we refer to Territorial Civilization, which is a structure-oriented, surface layer civilization; when we classify civilization in terms of custom, religion, and science, we refer to a culture-oriented, middle layer civilization. In contrast, Global Civilization reveals civilization through the understanding of human nature and the quest of humanity, so it is the core layer of civilization. Strictly speaking, the core layer civilization is Prime Civilization. Literally, Prime Civilization is the primary, fundamental and basic aspect of humanity—the unity of Human Nature and Race Nature, and the essence of life and being. Therefore, we say Prime Civilization is about the essence of humanity. It is the most fundamental, the most basic, and the most pervasive cultural concept. It is Prime Civilization that provides fertile soil for political, economic, scientific, moral, and spiritual civilizations.

As an indefinite concept, Global Civilization is defined from the perspective of human habitat. Civilization has its definite scale of effective scope that can be divided into three spheres. The first one is Small Civilization. The sphere of Territorial Civilizations, such as tribal civilization, Chinese, Hindu, Eastern, or Western civilizations, belongs to this category. The second one is Medium Civilization. The sphere of universal civilization is in this category when it refers to the whole human society or the notion of a world civilization. Regardless of the scale, Small or Medium Civilization is a notion narrowly applied to humanity, excluding its external environment. A third sphere of civilization comprises Small and Medium Civilizations as well as human environment, which is the cradle of humanity and platform of all human activity. This is a sphere of human environmental civilization in a much broader sense, including all human-related civilizations such as Alien Civilization, Outer Space Intelligence, biosphere, and possible pre-human civilization. In this sense, Global Civilization is human environmental civilization. Compared to Small and Medium Civilizations, obviously it is a

Greater Civilization. Greater Civilization accommodates and nourishes Small and Medium Civilizations, and Small and Medium Civilizations promote and elevate the Greater Civilization. Therefore, the Greater Civilization is the most profound, the most comprehensive, and the highest level of civilization. It is the foundation and fertile ground for the existence and growth of other spheres of civilizations, such as society civilization, ethnic civilization, national civilization, regional civilization, or human civilization.[9]

To join humanity to its environment on the one hand and environmental nature to humanity on the other is the true purpose of Global Civilization.

Using terms such as these, it is easy to get the impression that Global Civilization is the most general and common element in the civilization system. In fact, it is Global Civilization that constitutes the most prolific, most fundamental, and most profound part of the civilization system in the twenty-first century. For example, Global Civilization should encompass a full spectrum of new paradigms in the human governance system, including a new political system represented by a World Parliament, a World Government, and a World Judiciary Council; a new international law system with a World Constitution, the Law of World Military Force, the Law of Nation-State, the Law of Sovereignty Border, the Law of Head of State, the Law of World Citizen, and the Law of World Political Party as its building blocks; a new eco-environment governance system with emphasis on a sustainable global environment and scientific ecosystem management; a new economic system with a just and fair distribution of wealth and resource as its basic principle; a new religious system characterized by integrating the common rationale from major religious doctrines and practices; a new scientific and technological system with peaceful life and higher humanity as its purpose and standard; a new morality system with freedom of citizens, sovereignty of states, unity of the world, and Mutual development of humanity-universe as its key ingredient; a new cultural system featured by the benign interaction between indigenous and global cultures, between humanity and ecosystems, and between traditional and modern values; the list goes on. Therefore, Global Civilization "refers to a complex mix of

---

9   Prime Civilization and Greater Civilization form a unity. Prime Civilization is the holographic embryo for Global Civilization. Greater Civilization is a special branch of Global Civilization. Anything fundamental and deeply rooted is certainly universal and widely applicable. Anything pervasive and universal is certainly deeply rooted and fundamental. Whether the unity of Prime Civilization and Greater Civilization is achieved is an important benchmark to determine the level of civilization in history.

higher levels of morality, religion, learning, art, philosophy, technology, material well-being, and probably other things."[10]

If this is so, what we need today from political/religious leaders and business/academic elites in the twenty-first century is not their skill in maneuvering civilization clashes or their kindness to tolerate other cultures or their humbleness to learn from others or their courage to combat anti-civilized acts; we need a crucial paradigm shift in their minds, an uplifting of their own consciousness. They are expected to grasp the new learning course of Global Civilization sooner rather than later, starting from the very basics.

Furthermore, in one way or another, leaders are representatives elected by the public. So the most pressing issue in the twenty-first century is to educate humankind and raise public awareness of the spirit of Global Civilization. There have been two crucial learning periods throughout the five million years of human history. The first one was a learning period when humankind departed from animal kingdoms, when our ancestors learned how to walk upright, make and use tools, use fire, use language, learn social organization, and learn to be civilized. It was a phase of learning to becoming the human species, more or less, in a biological sense. The second one is a learning period for humankind in the twenty-first century—our responsibility—to learn equality, to learn world peace, to learn human righteousness, to learn universal truth, to learn the true meaning of humanity and self-governance, to learn how to be global citizens and children of the Earth, to learn how to promote civilization by civilized means. It is a critical period for human beings to learn how to be a unified human race in this universe. If we say that the first learning period was about how to be civilized within isolated societies, then the second period is about how to live in a civilized way in a global world. The fundamental course for this second learning period is Global Civilization.[11]

What are the curriculums that Global Civilization proposes?

First, every current civilization has features not only of distinctive individuality but also commonality that can be found among all civilizations. Only through this commonality are we able to understand and optimize the individuality. Only then are we able to resolve and eliminate conflicts between civilizations. This is

---

10   Huntington, S. P. (1996): The *Clash of Civilizations and the Remaking of World Order*. Simon & Schuster: New York. Page 320. Chapter 12. The West, Civilizations, and Civilization.

11   Indeed, the true understanding of civilization comes too late. Human beings have been struggling to reach it throughout ten thousand years of civilization history. Unfortunately, the extraordinary energy of civilization and the paramount creativity of human beings have been strictly confined within a narrow and sterile ground of state sovereignty, religious territory, and ethnic tradition for thousands of years. It was not until the last decade when humanity started to appreciate the concept of Global Civilization.

the only way to comply with the principle of promoting civilization by civilized means. **It is impossible to promote civilization by any uncivilized or anti-civilized means. This is the First and Foremost Experience of nearly 10,000 years of civilization history.**

Second, all current and past civilizations were produced in a tribal age, nation-state age, or region-centered age, so it is perfectly normal to have differences and conflicts between civilizations. Today, any act that guides difference and conflict towards violence and warfare—no matter what the reason used for justification—and any cultural penetration and civilization exportation by ways of economic sanction, political intimidation, or military intervention is nothing less than a direct anti-civilized deed. Therefore, **constraining the degree of conflict strictly to a nonviolent, non-force level is the First and Foremost Principle to be followed in the twenty-first century.**

Third, in a tribal era, the interest of the tribe is the highest; in a nation-state age, the interest of sovereign state is above all. In the twenty-first century, with increasing human integration, only the collective interest of the whole of humanity is the most fundamental welfare for every region, state, and individual. Therefore, **the interest of the whole of humanity is the First and Foremost Interest above all others.**

Fourth, humans are the crafted work of the universe, but not the gods and never the soul of the universe. Humans are children of the Earth, not the lords of all beings, and never the kings of the Earth. Humankind is a collective race, not just a group of social animals, and never a collection of solitary creatures. Other human beings are the true reflection of us, not our servants and never our enemies. The origin of brutality and arrogance is ignorance in humanity. Therefore, **to understand the true meaning of humanity is the First and Foremost Lesson humankind must humbly learn today.**

Fifth, all members of the human family, whether black, white, yellow, or red, male or female, young or old, share the same humanity. We are all equal. We all have the same needs. Therefore, the well-being of individuals is always fundamental to the whole of humanity. Conversely, humanity is a whole, integrated through individuals. The safety of the whole is always fundamental for any individual. In other words, Human Rights and Race Right are the two interconnected poles of the Humanity Rights system. Between these two poles are sovereignty rights, government rights, and civil rights, including the Right of Territory, the Right of Air Space, the Right of Ocean Space, the Right of Property, the Right of Military Commanding, etc. All these rights are supplementary to, and serve Human Rights and Race Right. Therefore, **all other rights must be subordinate to and serve Human Rights and Race Right. This is the First and Foremost Order for those decision-makers of all kinds of rights in human society in the twenty-first century.**

These five "first and foremost" principles are the fundamentals of Global Civilization.

3.   The Origin and Framework of Global Civilization

Humanity is composed of three key elements. The first element is material life, physiological and biological needs. The second is social life and emotional needs. The third is spirituality and spiritual needs. Similarly, civilization has three major components: its worldview and other derived forms; its view of humanity and other derived forms; its spirituality and other derived forms.

Throughout 10,000 years of civilization history, a number of distinctive civilizations have emerged from geographic isolation, such as the Near East and Northern African civilization, Hindu civilization, Sinic civilization, Jewish civilization, Islamic civilization, Western European civilization, Slavic civilization, African civilization, Japanese civilization, American civilization, Latin American civilization, Oceania civilization, etc. Each civilization expresses its people's understanding of the world, of humanity and of spirituality.

After a comprehensive analysis of the above civilizations from the perspectives of the global world and a collective humanity, we can summarize and extract from them three civilization systems that have the most representativeness and worldwide significance, and that are most likely critical contributors to guide humankind to a brighter future.

1. Western Civilization originated from the prehistoric Aegean, was shaped by ancient Greece and Rome, and matured through modern European and North American Civilization. This is a civilization system that emphasizes the relation between humans and nature, a model that promotes material well-being, respects the law of nature, and values scientific knowledge. Its primary achievement is the worldview of the concept of The Oneness of All Matter based on the unity of determinism and indeterminism.

2. Eastern Civilization originated from the Yellow River Civilization, was shaped by Taoism, Confucianism, and Buddhism, and matured through modern East Asian and South-East Asian Civilizations. This civilization system emphasizes the social relation in human society, a model that promotes righteousness and justice, pursues the unity of all peoples, and values humanity studies. Its primary achievement is the view of humanity as manifesting the concept of The Oneness of All Humans based on the unity of human naturality and morality.

3. Middle Civilization originated from ancient Egypt, was shaped by ancient Hebrew and Babylon Civilization, and matured through modern Judaism, Christianity, and Islamic civilizations. It is a civilization

system that emphasizes the relation between humans and the Creator, a model that promotes faith, reveres God, and values theology. Its primary achievement is a spirituality manifesting the concept of The Oneness of All Faiths based on the unity of the transcendent and ultimate nature of spirituality.

Interestingly, Blue Civilization has been a metaphor for Western Civilization, Yellow Civilization for Eastern, and Red Civilization for Middle. Indeed, it is the essence of these three great civilizations that composes the tricolor of Global Civilization.[12]

It is necessary to stress that any one of these—Western, Eastern, and Middle Civilizations—cannot be the dominant backbone in Global Civilization. To treat any one of them as the primary, will inevitably lead to cultural imperialism and cause new disaster to the human society. Narrow emphasis on one element of the trinity provokes the tendency to reject, play down, and misread the other two elements; such a narrow emphasis will eventually lead itself to the wrong side of its original emphasis. Additionally, while each civilization has beneficial elements that contribute to its greatness, none of them is free of defect: Western Civilization has the element of materializing humanity, Middle Civilization has the element of deifying humanity, and Eastern Civilization has the element of alienating humanity.

Therefore, we cannot ratify such claims as that the twenty-first century will be the century of the East[13] or the West, or the century of biology or of space sci-

---

12   It is necessary to further explain two points here. First, we all live on planet Earth. The Earth is round without artificial division of West or East. The term Western, Eastern and Middle Civilization is used here only because of the traditional definition of civilizations by geographical and territorial terms. In other words, our purpose is to thoroughly analyze major civilizations and extract essence from them as components for Global Civilization. Second, the phrases "emphasizes" and "primary achievement" are used to define the three major civilizations because each of them includes elements of the others, even though the element might be secondary and subordinate. For other civilizations, such as Hindu, Japanese, South American, African, and Oceania civilizations, it might not be appropriate to categorize them into any of these major civilizations in terms of geography and history. However, the civilization standard derived from the achievements of the three majors can be used to provide reasonable explanations for properties of other civilizations and provide basic guidance for their advancement.

13   In the twenty-first century, individuals, groups, nations, and states are increasingly globalized. The same is true for politics, economy, culture, and religion. In such a global world, it is extremely important to establish a universal principle to safeguard the global interaction. History is calling for a universal morality to embrace concepts like equality and universal brotherhood. Eastern civilization gets its name from its focus on a

ence. The fact that the twenty-first century is a global century with every aspect of human existence interconnected by globalization suggests that the twenty-first century can only be a century of collective development, a century of peace and equity, and a century of coordination and reciprocity. It must be a century of global development and civilized development. It must be a century to civilize every corner of the globe. Therefore, Global Civilization is a universal civilization. It is an entirely new form of civilization system that originates from and integrates the concept of three great civilizations, but it is independent of and transcends their achievements. In this system, the Western element emphasizes the natural, physical, and scientific needs of humanity; the Eastern element emphasizes the social, value-based, and moral needs of humanity; whereas the Middle element emphasizes the spiritual, faith-based, and self-actualization needs of humanity. Each element plays a vital role in distinct levels, mutually interconnected and reciprocally supportive as a trinity.

The boundless Blue Ocean is the birthplace of life, the origin of humanity. Over the horizon of the blue ocean, a magnificent Yellow Land, sheathed with fresh green, is the paradise for humankind. High above the Blue Ocean and the Yellow Land, a Red Sun, representing the Divine, is the Creator that shines its love, care, and guidance on human beings. The symbolic colors of blue, yellow, and red, the essence of nature, humanity, and divinity, the structure of body, mind, and spirit, the tendency of truth, goodness, and beauty are the three elements of civilization that mutually stimulate each other and animatedly echo in harmony. This is the picture of human society that Global Civilization is envisioning for the twenty-first century and the future.

In summary, the strengths of the Western, Eastern, and Middle Civilizations—the worldview of The Oneness of All Matter, the view of humanity of The Oneness of All Humans, the spirituality of The Oneness of All Faiths—are mutually sup-

---

social morality that promotes concepts such as "public spirit that rules all under the sky" and "selflessly serve the common good" throughout 5000 years of history. Many scholars around the world have now considered Eastern Civilization as the civilization for the global age. Scholars who have similar views are from the East (such as many Chinese scholars, led by Xianlin Ji), the West (such as Arnold Toynbee of the United Kingdom and many others from the West), as well as from the Middle (such as many Israeli and Iranian scholars). However in a deeper level, from long-term holistic perspective, people in a global world should never underestimate the significance of material life, physical needs, and scientific spirit emphasized by the West. Similarly, humanity will not be sustained for a moment without the spirituality and faith emphasized by the Middle. Therefore, the concept of the twenty-first century as a century of the East is by no means beneficial to humankind or to any part of the whole.

portive, complementary, and elevating as a trinity. They construct the solid framework of Global Civilization.

II. Further Analysis

Civilization, generally speaking, refers to the concept of human existence in certain times. The concept of human existence comprises three basic aspects, namely a thinking concept, a behavior concept, and a faith concept. The thinking concept expresses a corresponding worldview. The behavior concept expresses a corresponding outlook on humanity. The faith concept expresses a corresponding spirituality.

Further, civilization is the result that evolved from its embryo. The embryo of a new civilization is always created in a civilization system that is relatively mature and gradually outmoded. Once a civilization system is no longer appropriate for the scope of interaction and the level of self-consciousness of its people, the embryo of a new civilization is created. When the embryo rapidly grows and penetrates the entire body of the society, including political, economical, cultural, and social realms, a new civilization system conditioned by its embryo is then born.[14]

As an embryo of a new civilization for humanity, Global Civilization has already been presented to us in real life. This is the worldview of The Oneness of All Matter provided by Western Civilization, the humanity outlook of The Oneness of All Humans provided by Eastern Civilization, the spirituality of The Oneness of All Faiths provided by Middle Civilization.

1   The Concept of The Oneness of All Matter

Just as animal survival is determined by food availability, humankind's social life is determined by people's thinking. The most essential thinking is our view towards the world in which we live.

The core of worldview is philosophy. The level of philosophical thinking reflects the cognitive capability to perceive the world. It has often been stated by philosophers that the quality of a nation depends on its level of philosophical

---

14   Similarly, an embryo of a new civilization has three integrated parts. First, the worldview it provides; second, the humanity outlook it supports; and third, the spirituality that it implies. These three parts constitute a unified DNA Segment, which determines the characteristic of a forthcoming civilization.

thinking. Plato, the father of Western philosophy, went further and claimed in his Republic that qualified rulers must be philosopher kings.

There is a definite pattern of worldview evolution: from surface to depth, from direct to underlying. Why do we even exist? We exist because premises and historical/current conditions bring us into being. Then why were these premises and conditions established? If we continue asking questions like this, eventually we will arrive the domain of searching the first cause. This is the basic logical questioning that defines thinking. Following this logic, deterministic worldviews, such as ancient totemism, atomism, ontology, and causality, came into being naturally.

After millennia seeking the origin and first cause without success, humankind started to question the objectives and methods of this endeavor and shifted to a very different focus on real objects and specific matters: How does one, or a nation, exist and behave? How does one particular object exist and behave? It is in the process of discovering these specifics that cognition of the innate structure and laws of motion for a specific object come about and thus science, in its strictest sense, came into being. The limitation of this approach is that it ignores the inner relation between the studied object and other objects; it excludes the inner relation between the studied object and humanity, and between the studied object and the essence of the universe—the ultimate existence. In addition, in a period of explosive growth of science/technology, positivism and increasing disciplinary specialization also played their part in bringing indeterministic worldviews into modern and contemporary times, such as random theory, quantum mechanics, probability theory, chaos theory, virtual theory, and self-organization theory.

Indeterministic theory does nothing to eliminate the problematic aspect of deterministic views; it actually denies its rational aspect altogether. Similarly, deterministic theory is unable to explain the rationality of indeterminism and is incapable of challenging its irrationality. Painful reflection upon this paradox leads people to a realization: both determinism and indeterminism have neglected the two-way relationship between objects, between the object and the cause, between the object and potentiality, and between the object and the future. They all fail to apprehend that relation is not only a nexus[15], a field, but also a force existence, an energy; they are unable to master that any relationship is two-way and the property of each way is different; they fail to understand that the difference between the two-way properties within the same relation is the origin of all events. Failing to adopt this relationship thinking is the very reason that the two

---

15   A. N. Whitehead's term and concept is used here as "a set of actual entities in the unity of the relatedness constituted by their prehensions of each other, or—what is the same thing conversely expressed—constituted by their objectifications in each other."— translator

opposite, but equally one-sided, worldviews of determinism and indeterminism came into being in ancient and modern times.

In fact, any discipline other than philosophy normally is a study of a real or putative object. Only philosophy, by providing a worldview as its mission, focuses on the study of relationship. Every goal of philosophy—such as seeking essence, truth, and law; acquiring wisdom, enlightenment, and spiritual fulfillment—can only exist within the interactive environment of relations. As soon as one is embarking on relation studies, one is in the territory of philosophy and the domain of worldview thinking. Since relations are not concrete matters or events that can be easily traced or observed, philosophy has inherited a speculative and abstract nature. In fact, the dynamic nature of all things can only be revealed through their relationships to each other. Thus, a relation carries all the codes and controls all the energy of the studied object.

From this relationship point of worldview, all things are created from relation, exist in relation, and end in relation. In other words, everything essentially is an intermediary agent, an object that is interwoven in a world of relatedness. Thus, all objects are determined and counterdetermining. Why does one thing exist and why does it behave the way it does? It is brought into being by the interaction between numerous things prior to its existence; once it is created, it is interacting with all existing things around it; it will continue to develop in a way determined by its nature through the interaction with things around it. This gives an object the inherent determinacy that defines itself, a determinacy decided by its unique prehistory, history, present, and future. If everything is merely determined, however, it would be timeless, motionless, and lifeless. It would be useless to others and valueless to itself. Indeed, the creation of a new thing is also the result of counterdeterministic action from the new element of the old system applying to all existing things around it. Once it is created, it is in the counterdeterministic relation with all existing things around it. Therefore, everything has an inherent counterdeterminacy towards its determinator in the old system and to all determinators around it. It certainly is counteracting with all determinators as a counterdeterminator. This action, whether to determinators or to counterdeterminators, is no doubt counterdeterministic.

The intrinsic dynamic of the determinacy of all things is their counterdeterminacy; the inherent premise of the counterdeterminacy of all things is their determinacy. Determinacy and counterdeterminacy are simply two properties of the same relation. These two are one—a wholeness of Determine-Counterdeterminacy. A determinator can be a determinator only when it exists within relation of numerous counterdeterministic elements and carries the element of counterdeterminacy. Similarly, a counterdeterminator can be a counterdeterminator only when it acts strictly within the provision limited by determinators. In other words, all things have the Determine-Counterdeterminacy, real and concrete, which defines their existence and makes them what they are. The Determine-Counterdeterminacy decides the relationship between all things in the universe and determines the relationship between all elements in everything in the following aspects:

1. In terms of intrinsic structure, it behaves the Law of the Interpenetration of Opposites, the Law of the Yin and Yang that mutually consumes and generates.
2. In terms of a developing process, it behaves the Law of the Transformation of Quantity into Quality and vice visa, the Law of the Negation of the Negation.
3. In terms of form of appearance, it behaves the Law of Action and Reaction.

Thus, determinacy apart from Determine-Counterdeterminacy is a dried river. Similarly, counterdeterminacy without the Determine-Counterdeterminacy is a stagnant pond. Likewise, any dialectics without the Determine-Counterdeterministic principle would be arbitrary juggles, and their contradictory principles would inevitably be fallacies. Moreover, without applying Determine-Counterdeterministic thinking, it is not possible to arrive at an objective understanding of the fundamental existence in the universe, such as substance, motion, field, space, and time.

Clearly, Determine-Counterdeterminism as a new philosophical thinking and worldview not only reveals the essence of all things, the property of relation, the cause and the dynamic of motion, and the law and direction of development but it also reflects the cosmic essence and the spirit of the universe underlying all things given by the Creator. It makes the most fundamental issues of the world clear:

1. Because of determinacy, all things and the Cosmos manifest inevitability, certainty, unity, orderliness, uniformity, and directionality.
2. Because of the co-existing counterdeterminacy, all things and the Cosmos also reveal activeness, novelty, potentiality, divergence, and multidirectionality.
3. It is at the focal point of interaction and convergence between determinacy and counterdeterminacy that: the universe is created; the cause, dynamic, boundary, limit, law, and direction of all things and the Cosmos are set, thus form the cosmic structure and its unity, activeness, and dynamic; and the space/time, which puzzled humankind for so many years, is born.

For example, Einstein's relativity theory is a significant milestone in the human quest to the ultimate knowledge because his special theory of relativity has revealed the true relation of Determine-Counterdeterminacy between mass, energy, speed, time, and space in a special reference system; his general theory of relativity has revealed the true relation of Determine-Counterdeterminacy in a general reference system.[16]

The significance of Determine-Counterdeterminism is apparent. First, the direct and superficial mode of thinking that views the relation of all things merely as interrelating and interacting has been widely adopted throughout history.

---

16 Einstein's theory of relativity is neither determinism nor indeterminism; however, it is the closest theory to Determine-Counterdeterminism so far.

For the first time in history, the theory of relativity proves, in mathematical terms from the perspective of physics, that determinacy and deterministic action have a property of relativity due to counterdeterminacy and counterdeterministic action. Likewise, counterdeterminacy and counterdeterministic action have a property of relativity due to determinacy. Therefore, relativity is the physical form and appearance of Determine-Counterdeterminacy. Determine-Counterdeterminism, in fact, is the underlying law and essence of relativity. It is correct to say that everything shows special and general relativity because it's Determine-Counterdeterminacy, but it would be false to claim that its relativity causes its Determine-Counterdeterminacy. This irreversibility logically suggests that the theory of relativity has only answered the question of "Is it relative or not?" In contrast, Determine-Counterdeterminism addresses issues such as "To whom is it relative?" (In terms of physics and appearance, it shows relativity between mass, energy, speed, space and time of an object just as the theory of relativity suggests. At a deeper level, it shows that the determinacy and deterministic action from the determinator to the determined is relative, and the counterdeterminacy and counterdeterministic action from the counterdeterminator to the determinator is relative). "How do they relate to each other?" (The determinator encompasses the determined. The counterdeterminacy and counterdeterministic action from the counterdeterminator can only work within the provision confined by its determinator). "Why are they relative?" (The determinator can only exist with its counterdeterminator as premise so determinacy has the underlying premise of counterdeterminacy. Therefore the determinacy and deterministic action of the determinator to its counterdeterminator is relative. Since the counterdeterministic action from the counterdeterminator cannot just react and counteract freely, it must be confined within the provision set by the determinator. So the counterdeterminacy and counterdeterministic action of the counterdeterminator is also relative).

More importantly, while relativity presents a relative paradigm for the world of physics, Determine-Counterdeterminism provides a dynamic and definite worldview for the universe. It is a Determine-Counterdeterministic, a Super-deterministic, and a Self-deterministic worldview that integrates cognitive concepts from Einstein's relativity, Newton's absolutism, Bohr's quantum theory, Godel's incompleteness Theorem, Steven Hawking's theory about black holes, Goldbach's conjecture, Hegel's absolute concept, and Lao-zi's Taoism. It reveals the origin of the universe, the root of the universe order, the soul of cosmic evolution, and the ultimate destiny of the universe.

Determine-Counterdeterminism has departed from this mode and establishes a thinking which reveals that the relation of things should strictly follow Determine-Counterdeterministic law—a law of mutual corroboration and mutual support that demonstrates the inherent law and the underlying orderliness of things. That is to say, to understand and master a matter is a journey of identifying its various determinators and counterdeterminators and discovering the Determine-Counterdeterministic relation between all parties. For example, father and son, according to the Determine-Counterdeterministic principle, are determined by factors such as species property, historical condition, social situation, family structure, etc. Simultaneously, they are counterdetermining these deterministic factors at all times through Determine-Counterdeterministic action. Only so can they come to being, can they communicate and develop. Counterdeterminators keep defining their nature and regularity through numerous determinators, whereas determinators keep adopting novelty and possibility from counterdeterminators. Determinators and counterdeterminators are mutually corroborating in a benign way. What a perfect universe order it is! As a structural principle revealing the essence of the universe, Determine-Counterdeterminism has presented humanity with a vision of an orderly life, an orderly society, and an orderly universe.

Second, a revolutionary mode of thinking that views the relation of all things as unity of opposites, negation of the negation, and so on, has been adopted for centuries. Determine-Counterdeterminism has departed from this mode and establishes a way of thinking which reveals that the relation of things should strictly follow the Determine-Counterdeterministic law—a law of mutual relating and mutual complementing that demonstrates harmony and co-existence. In other words, to understand and master a matter is a journey of discovering the underlying corridor of harmony and mechanism of co-existence between determinators and counterdeterminators. According to the Determine-Counterdeterministic principle, father and son are by no means in a relation of opposite unity, or negation of the negation. Quite the contrary, they can only be in a mutually complementary relation that manifests mutual corroboration, mutual reciprocity, and mutual supplementation; they can only be in a relation of affirmation of the affirmation, which manifests mutual loving, mutual generating, and co-existing. Counterdeterminators keep receiving care and nutrition from numerous determinators, while determinators keep receiving respect and satisfaction from counterdeterminators. Determinators and counterdeterminators are mutually complementing in a benign way. What a harmonious picture of the universe it is! As a law of process revealing the essence of the universe, Determine-Counterdeterminism has presented humanity with a vision of a harmonious life, a harmonious society, and a harmonious universe.

Third, the negative and pessimistic mode of thinking that views the relation of things as mutually constraining and mutually damaging has been adopted for centuries. Determine-Counterdeterminism has departed from this mode and establishes a thinking which reveals that the relation between things should strictly follow the law of Determine-Counterdeterminism—a law of mutual promoting and mutual creating that demonstrates positivenesss and creativeness. According to the Determine-Counterdeterministic principle, one can always find that father and son are marching side by side on the broad road of positivenesss and creativeness. The actual cause of many unfortunate cases of mutual damage is derived from the outmoded thinking mentioned above. Counterdeterminators keep getting support and momentum from numerous determinators, while determinators keep getting newness and vitality from counterdeterminators. Determinators and counterdeterminators are mutually interacting in a benign way. What a vivid vision of the universal it is! As a law of evolution and development revealing the essence of the universe, Determine-Counterdeterminism has presented humanity with a vision of a positive life, a positive society, and a positive universe.

Hence, Determine-Counterdeterminacy is not only the Cosmic Cause that creates the Universe, but also the Cosmic Soul that defines the orderliness of the Universe. Moreover, it is the Cosmic Effect that sets the destination of the universe's evolution. Indeed, all beings in the universe are no more than three forms of existence: material energy, field energy, and spiritual energy. That is to say, all things and the universe are essentially energy; energy is essentially an "Orderly Kinetic State" with Determine-Counterdeterminacy.

In short, all things have Determine-Counterdeterminacy and are within the orderly web of Determine-Counterdeterministic relatedness; therefore, the universe is an organic whole and all things are interconnected as one. The notion of oneness used in the phrase "The Oneness of All Matter" refers to the Determine-Counterdeterminacy that permeates all things, defines their existence, relation, and development. Since all things have Determine-Counterdeterminacy and are within the interwoven Determine-Counterdeterministic interactions, so all things are distinctive but related, independent, but mutually generating. It is clear that Determine-Counterdeterminism inherits rationality from both the determinism and the indeterminism of the past. It has avoided common pitfalls in traditional worldviews such as the one-sided logic, the exclusive model, the materialistic framework, and the ontological habit, and has embraced rational principles of worldview approaches, such as achieving cognition through relation, searching for truth within relation, and discovering the future within relation. Therefore, we say that Determine-Counterdeterminism is a new thinking, a new worldview extracted from the fruit of Western Civilization, especially from schools of Determinism and Indeterminism in Western philosophy and science.

"The Oneness of All Matter" means everything forms oneness with any other thing. At a deeper level, it implies that all things share one essence.

We believe that the relation-oriented principle of Determine-Counterdeterminism, manifesting The Oneness of All Matter, is the world-view that Western Civilization has contributed to Global Civilization.

2.   The Concept of The Oneness of All Humans

Our view of humanity determines our idea of human existence. People's self-awareness is the origin of human activity, value orientation, and social behavior. It seems that the two millennia old proverb "Know thyself" has had no practical significance until today.

Then what exactly is humanity? The difficulty in reaching a true understanding lies in the method and reference frame that we use to comprehend and interpret humanity. For centuries, people have been defining humanity by comparing it with animals or the Creator/deity, and in reference frames of human derivatives, such as family, society, state, culture, or religion. Thus, it was natural to draw the following conclusions during the developing process of the history of human self-understanding:

1.   Humans are animal beings, without feathers, with intelligence and emotion and who walk upright.

2.   Humans are divine beings with a cultural, political, and social nature, the masters of the world.

3.   Humans are monsters, half angels and half beasts.

In fact, neither can we fly to the heavenly kingdom to comprehend the divine, nor can we crawl into the world of jungle to appreciate animals. It is a critical logical mistake to define humanity by comparing it with other beings that we hardly understand. Likewise, it makes no sense to define humanity in a reference frame of human derivatives. These derivatives, as products of human activity, are simply outward forms of human self-awareness in a certain stage in history. An original cannot be defined through its derivatives. False logic inevitably leads to wrong deductions. Therefore, the conclusions that equate a human being with an animal being, with a divine being, and with a monster are all groundless.

This means that we can properly define humanity only by the relation-oriented worldview and a Determine-Counterdeterministic way of thinking, that is, to appreciate humanity within the Determine-Counterdeterministic relations between animal, human, and the Creator; we can clearly appreciate humanity only through the reference frame of Universe Essence, which creates humanity and gives us Human Essence, that is, to appreciate humanity through the appreciation of the Universe Essence within ourselves. If so, a very simple but profound fact is presented: the essence of humanity is Naturality-Morality[17].

A human is born in nature, inhabits nature, and ceases to exist in nature. So humanity has intrinsic natural essence—naturality. Humanity also carries an animal birthmark because it was created in nature after other animal species were created. The human's natural essence and the form of animal are the premise, the substratum, and the vehicle that regulate and sustain humanity. However, once humankind leaves the animal world and becomes a unique biological species, it starts to strongly reject its animality from a higher perspective. In order to be free from animality, humankind has found and established a higher existence according to human apprehension of the first cause and to the experience of searching the human essence. Through faith in the higher power, the human race was able to enter the gateway of humanity. It is a profound accomplishment which differentiates humans from animals.

It should be asserted that humans' naturality and morality is an integral whole of Naturality-Morality. Only moralized naturality can be humanity, otherwise it will be animality. Likewise, only naturalized morality can be humanity, otherwise it will be divinity. We can also say that deified animality, or animalized divinity is humanity. The special species on earth with animality-humanity-divinity trinity is humanity. If an academic term is needed in philosophy, anthropology, cultural studies, and humanity studies, then *humanity* may be defined as "a biological being on earth with Naturality-Morality." Naturality-Morality is the human form of the Universe Essence. In the same way, the Universe Essence reflects in a rock as basic existence, reflects in a vegetable life as general growth, and reflects in an animal life as biological/physical activity.

In the earlier section, we defined humanity as the unity of Human Nature and Race Nature; human existence as the unity of individuals and the collective whole; human evolution as the mutual cohering of humanity and its environment. The concept that humanity is Naturality-Morality is the reason behind all these definitions. That is to say, Naturality-Morality is the common origin of humanity (unity of Human Nature and Race Nature), of the human existence (unity of individuality and collectivity), and of the human evolution (unity of humanity and environment).

What is the conclusion of the above analysis? It proclaims:

- We are humans, not animals. We should not define humanity as animality governed by laws of the jungle.

---

17 The translation "Morality" refers to properties that humanity possesses apart from its natural aspects. It includes human's awareness, morality, and cultural/social aspects.—translator.

- We are humans, not the divine. We should not define humanity as divinity that dominates the Universe above all beings.
- We are humans, not monsters. We should not define humanity as a monster that is sometimes like an angel and sometimes like a beast.
- We are humans; human can only be human. We are simply earthly creatures: moralized natural beings and naturalized moral beings.

We can further analyze this in a chronological sense. Humanity is very different from the animal or the Divine in the sense that only human beings need two creation processes. A tree or a cat lives its life from birth to death without essential change; a divine being worshipped by any faith is eternal and immortal. In contrast, human beings have to experience Spontaneous Creation and Conscious Creation processes to become human beings.

This can be exemplified by the growth process of individuals: every normal person should experience two creation processes, and each process has two phases of growth.

In the first phase of the first creation, the person acquires a physical body from his or her parents and nature. This body is the vehicle, the premise, and the basis to being a human being. This phase includes the period of conception, embryo, and infancy. The second phase is to acquire human quality and individuality from family and society through social interaction and education. This phase includes periods of childhood, teenage years, and youth. After this phase, one has advanced from a natural human being to a normal human being.

The second creation has greater significance. During the first phase of this creation, one comprehends and applies Human Nature, Race Nature, and their relation; observes and appreciates the relationship with fellow humans, with the Creator, and the relationship of one's body and mind; and consciously self-transforms to a human being who governs oneself by proper moral consciousness, who contributes to society and achieves self-actualization. This phase includes periods of middle age and late-middle age. The second phase comes when one approaches a mature understanding and mastery upon aging and death—an understanding that comprehends one's late years as the most mature and meaningful stage in life with paramount responsibility of education; an understanding that views death as the most profound transformation, mission, duty, contribution, new birth, and eternity in one's life, in humanity, and in the universe.[18]

Thus, if the first creation of individual human being can be considered as accomplishing the life mission of "human does not equal animal," then the sec-

---

18   The reason why those outstanding individuals in history show extraordinary characters and noble personality is that, after experiencing the first creation from Natural Human Beings to Normal Human Beings, they all accomplished the second creation advancing from Spontaneous Human Beings to Conscious Human Beings.

ond creation of the individual can be termed as taking the leap to "human equals human."

The growth process of the human race is the same.

At the end of the twentieth century, humankind entered a global world and an information age. The lengthy period in history before this point can be categorized as the first creation, the spontaneous creation process. Four million years of primitive history belongs to the first phase of this creation. About the last 5000 years of civilization history, more significantly the two millennia from 1000 BCE to 1000 CE, constitutes the second phase. After the second phase, the human race was able to walk upright, use tools, fire, and language, learned legal matters and culture, consciously socialize, and so on. It is the creation of humankind as one Natural species—the creation of the "Human".

It is increasingly evident that humankind is now entering into the second creation process since the end of the twentieth century. It is the creation of a unique collective existence in the universe—the creation of the "Race."

After experiencing the first phase of the second creation, the human race will be freed from the constraint and dominance of partial thinking—such as individual-oriented, group-oriented, kinship-oriented, clan-oriented, and ethnic-oriented and consciously come to the realization that humanity is a collective existence; hence, everybody will be able to think, work, and interact in accordance with our Race Nature. The key mission in this phase, as discussed earlier, is to learn and master equality, peace, and unity; to learn to be qualified global citizens and children of the Earth; learn and embrace Global Civilization and to promote civilization by civilized means. It is no doubt one of the most crucial events in human evolution and an exciting quantum leap in the cosmic development. Obviously, the first phase of the second creation is a period of "humanity consciously becoming a collective race."

Thereafter, humanity needs to embark on another mission assigned by the spirit of the universe—to complete the second phase of the second creation, a phase of humanity consciously self-negating its Race Nature. In this phase, by consciously following the evolutional direction of Naturality-Morality, with the humble willingness of self-negation, through human wisdom and endeavor, humanity will self-transform into a superhuman being, thus leading the cosmic evolution and human civilization to a higher level—the Superhuman stage of the cosmic evolution. This self-negating process is the highest human mission assigned by the Universe, the highest human pride, and the highest level of evolution.

Recent developments in science, technology, and philosophy have already sparked encouraging signs of the emergence of a higher species. There has been, for instance, progress made in DNA sequencing, genetic modifying technology, stem cell research, telomere technology, clone technology, theoretical physics, high-energy physics, UFO research, and space technology. More significantly, we are reaching deeper understanding of the origin of the universe, its structural mechanism, the law of evolution, the ultimate destination, and the universal spirit that permeates the entire universe; people are awakening to a sense of responsibility for the self-evolution process, for the progress of earth civilization, and for the development of the universe. This has signified the brilliant creation process.

If we say the first creation of the human race is to achieve the progress of "humanity does not just equal Homo Sapiens," then the second creation is to accomplish the solemn mission of "humanity equals a collective race."

In summary, there is only one human race on this planet, so we should be united; we all share one nature, so everybody should be equal. There is only one Earth, so we should treasure it. We can only have one life, so we should be serious about it. The life span is one blinking moment, so we should cherish it. All these "ones" prompt humankind today to the philosophy of The Oneness of All Humans.[19] That all humans share one nature is fundamental among these "ones". The notion "oneness" in the phrase "The Oneness of All Humans" refers to the Naturality-Morality that defines humankind. The fact that every human being has the same Naturality-Morality implies that there is only one way to save humankind from the chaos world—a way of equality, cooperation, unity, and harmony, a way of "What one recognizes as desirable for oneself, one ought to be willing to grant to others," "Do not to others what you do not want done to yourself," "One must always treat others just as one would want others to treat you." The concept of Naturality-Morality is the new philosophy extracted from the fruit of Eastern Civilization, particularly from Taoism, Confucianism, and Buddhism—those ancient ideas of "the Way is natural" and "humanity is benevolence"

The Oneness of all humans, generally speaking, means that every human being forms oneness with any other human being. At a deeper level, it implies that all peoples share one nature.

19　If so, most of the current and historical humanity outlooks are alienated and fallacious. The alienation and fallacy leads to a concrete result—humanity today could be considered as the most stupid and barbarous species on Earth. This can be exemplified by the fact that the nuclear arsenal in the world today has the capacity to destroy the six billion people 60 times! This is not only undeniable fact but also a violation of basic logics such as "Humanity is not created to be destroyed" or "Human life can only experience one death." Other examples are: the arms race—the competition of killing capacity—now becoming the dominant aspect in international relations; mammonism, eroticism, and destruction becoming a tripod that sustains human existence; he who has the money can place orders to politicians and military commanders, hire philosophers and theologians. The list goes on.

We believe that the principle based on unity of all peoples, the concept of Naturality-Morality manifesting The Oneness of All Humans, is the philosophy that Eastern Civilization has contributed to Global Civilization.

3. The Concept of The Oneness of All Faiths

The physical body is one's vehicle, society is the intermediate, and the spirit is one's essence or primary existence.[20] The core of the human spirit is one's faith

---

20   The understanding of "the physical body is one's vehicle, society is one's intermediate, the spirit is one's essence" is the single most important benchmark to evaluate the maturity of human consciousness. Centered on the subject of physical body, a large society of natural scientists has been formed; centered on the subject of society, a large group of politicians and social scientists has been formed; centered on the subject of spirit, a large community of psychologists as well as theologians/religionists has been formed. However, it is not difficult to find that these groups of theorists and practitioners either cut off the intrinsic interconnectedness of body, society, and spirit or misread, or even misplace, the position of the vehicle, the intermediate, and the essence, and thus mislead human consciousness towards faulty ground and create endless tragedies in human society.

We believe the essential reason that humanity is fundamentally different from, and superior to, animals is not only because humanity has a complex and sophisticated society and lives in it as the intermediate, but also, more profoundly, because humanity has reversed The primary/secondary position of the animal's mind-body relationship and chosen the biological evolution path with spirit as its essence. The Creator did not create human beings to destroy the nature or kill each other in a manner more brutal than animals, but for the following two purposes: (1) to raise the universe evolution to a higher level through this intelligent creature with spirit as its essence. That is, to develop to a higher level of biological conscious evolution from physical spontaneous evolution of the universe, (2) to reveal the truth of the universe that is hidden deep in the cosmos: material energy is the universe vehicle; field energy is the universe intermediate; spiritual energy is the universe essence.

From the moment the Universe was created (to eternity), it has been manifesting a nature with material energy as its vehicle, with field energy as its intermediate, and spiritual energy as its essence. If the Universe Spirit—the universe spiritual energy—was not the leading force and the essence of the universe's evolution, then it is unlikely the universe and all things have such perfect structure, such orderly process, and such definite purpose. The component of body/society/spirit and the structure of vehicle/intermediate/essence are simply the human form of the universe component (material energy, field energy, and spiritual energy) and universe structure (material energy as the vehicle, field energy as the intermediate, spiritual energy as the essence). Further analysis of this point is followed in latter paragraphs and in the footnote in the Conclusion section.

and belief that determines people's comprehension of the world in which we live, and of humanity. Worldview is the physical form of spirituality, and one's view of humanity is the psychological/moral form of spirituality. Because of this, most people have a common and profound feeling: the saddest thing in life is living without faith, the worst tragedy in life is falling into false worship, and the worst crime committed in life is using and abusing faith.[21]

The object of any faith is supernatural, supreme, ultimate, and unique existence, whether for faiths of a personal power, such as ancestor worship, hero worship, and seer worship, or for faiths of a proposition, such as totemism, ethnical worship, and ideological worship. It is always a divine being that controls humans, makes them venerated, and provides purpose and hope to their lives. In other words, it is a spiritual existence that creates, transcends, orchestrates, and protects human beings.

The direct reflection of people's spirituality is one's spiritual stature. Human spiritual stature is the standard to judge the maturity of one's self-consciousness, the standard to measure the purity of one's humanity, the standard to determine one's understanding of the Universe, and the originator of one's broadmindedness.[22]

Logically, humans' spiritual stature should be at such a level that their thoughts, words, pursuits and acts all qualify them as humans. That is to say, people should have a proper level of understanding of humanity and of humanity's place in the

---

21   It should be stressed that conflict caused by self-centered interest is at the surface layer whereas the cultural difference is at the middle layer, and faith-based clashing is at the core. It could be asserted that religious faith has the power not only to determine the political, economical, and ecological well-being of its faithful followers but also to shape the population density, human consciousness, and even properties of human species.

22   It is common place in today's world for people's spiritual stature to be at minimal, even below subsistence, levels. For instance, in some Western countries, freedom is perceived by some as the freedom to do whatever pleases themselves and whatever hurts others; equality is perceived by some as equally going to the two extremes, going into a split personality. In some Eastern countries, morality is treated as a strict sense of rules of conduct in terms of kinship hierarchy while personal feeling and emotion are taken over by kinship affinity, nativism, and ethnocentrism. Some religions label their purposes as salvation for all peoples but actually are conducting barbarian acts of hatred and killing. For some people, the spiritual stature is considered as nothing larger than the size of their own bedrooms and as something that should not be less than a pile of bank notes. Philosophers seem noble when, in fact, most of them are interested in their own emotional satisfaction and personal fulfillment only; some turn into manipulating tools to endorse politicians' policy. Politicians seem to have high levels of consciousness when, in fact, the true concern of many of them is their own ego and power.

universe to deserve the name of human; people should have a proper level of behavior in the full spectrum of social interaction between individuals, between societies, and between states to deserve the name of human; people should have a proper level of behavior in environmental interactions with ecological systems and social/psychological environments to deserve the name of human; people should have a proper level of behavior in handling relationships between body and spirit, between desire and righteousness, and between emotion and intellect to deserve the name of human.

Then how does one deserve the name of "human"? "How" is essentially a question of "Why". "Why" is essentially a question of "What is humanity?" "What is humanity?" is essentially a question of "Why should humanity behave this way?" Therefore, the fundamental question is: "What is the relation between humanity and the Creator, between humanity and the universe nature that gives us human nature, and between humanity and the world in which we live?"

Humanity was created by the Universe in the light of its spirit during the cosmic evolution process after an inorganic stage, an organic stage, and an animal stage. It is a new stage of life-being, a stage of human body-mind existence, a stage of Naturality-Morality. That is to say, our physical body is the evolved product of the universe in accordance with its spirit. So are our minds—the body-mind system of humanity with Determine-Counterdeterminacy and Naturality-Morality is one of evolved products of the universe spirit in the cosmic evolution.

This brings up the concept of the Universe Spirit. In its evolutionary process, the universe has demonstrated a mighty force, a profound character, and a great will. This force, character, and will can be deducted by the logical reasoning of philosophers, measured by the instruments of scientists, sensed by the intuition of theologians, and perceived by the experiences of laymen. Scientists define this force, character, and will as axioms, principles, theorems, and laws. Theologians revere it as God, Allah, Buddha, or Tao. Philosophers name it as the existence of the existence, the thought of the thought, the moral of the morality, and the freedom of the freedom. Laymen explain it as nature, the law of nature, or the way of the universe.

From the perspective of modern cognitive knowledge, this Universe Force, Universe Character, and Universe Will that underlies the entire cosmic evolution is an existence with the nature of ultimate spiritual reality and of the Universe Spirit. Universe Force is the momentum, the driving force and the structural strength behind the evolution process. Universe Character unifies all things in the universe. It not only unifies planes of macroscopic and microscopic, spheres of distant and proximate, and realms of the highest and the lowest, but it also unifies cause and effect, singularity and multiplicity, physic and metaphysic in the universe. Universe Will is the certainty with which the universe regulates its existence, the novelty that activates, awakens, and develops the potentiality and possibility of everything during its interaction with others. It is the transcendence that enables everything to continuously exceed itself through interaction with others. The unity of this Universe Force, Universe Character, and the Universe Will is the Universe Spirit.[23] This Universe Spirit is precisely the God or Holy Spirit that has been revered by human beings throughout history. It is the God of Christianity, the Allah of Islam, the Buddha of Buddhism, and the Way of Taoism.

Universe Spirit is not only the ignition and the engine but also the steering wheel and the road map of a profound cosmic evolution. Under the action of multiple forces from the Universe Spirit, the Universe produced the Earth four billion years ago. It nourished the first biological life on Earth about three billion years ago. It created Homo Sapiens, the only intelligent species known so far, about five million years ago. It gave birth to human civilization, which indicates the formation of human society, 10,000 years ago. Today, it once again sets the evolutional direction towards the maturity of humanity—towards Global Civilization.

Albert Einstein said, "I believe in Spinoza's God who reveals himself in the orderly harmony of what exists, not in a God who concerns himself with the fates and actions of human beings." He also stressed in his later years, "My religiosity

---

23   Yes, the universe has a spirit. The human spirit essentially is a special form of the Universe Spirit as the human spiritual state. A spirit is a power (or energy) with consciousness, self-awareness, cognitive ability, self-knowing ability, and self-acting ability. The universe must have a spirit to sustain itself otherwise it could not be created as an actual reality, unable to exist as an orderly system, and it would be impossible to evolve into an orderly process. Universe Spirit is also the only, the supreme, and the ultimate being; otherwise it would not have the power to create all beings and determine everything, and thus would not qualify the name of God or Allah.

Indeed, God, or Allah, is worshipped as the Creator and/or ruler because God, or Allah, represents the mind of the Cosmos, the spirit of the Universe. From the spiritual perspective, the universe is an energy system that is regulated and determined by its spirit. From the Cosmology perspective, the Universe Spirit is the mind of the universe that orchestrates the working mechanism of the cosmic process. It is indeed the essence of the universe, the fundamental essence of the Cosmos. The universe would be an inanimate world without its spirit. Similarly, the spirit, if isolated from the meaningful cosmic context, would be a groundless assumption and wild illusion by human's limited knowledge. The Universe Spirit, in short, is the unity of the spiritual Cosmos and the dominant spirit of the Universe; we can name it as Universe-Spirit.

From another perspective, just as only laws of physics can explain physical reaction, only laws of chemistry can explain chemical reaction, only spiritual laws can explain spiritual phenomenon. Hence it is possible to explain the human spirit only by the Universe Spirit because human spirit in essence is a product of universe evolution in a certain stage. It is essentially a human form of the Universe Spirit.

consists of a humble admiration for an infinitely superior spirit that reveals itself in the little that we can comprehend of the knowable world. That deeply emotional conviction of the presence of a superior reasoning power, which is revealed in the incomprehensible universe, forms my idea of God." Renowned historian Arnold Toynbee asserted that there is an "ultimate spiritual reality in and behind the Universe in which Man finds himself." He also pointed out that for five seers, namely Zarathustra, Deutero-Isaiah, Gautama, Confucius, and Pythagoras, the most momentous common feature in them "is the attainment, by an individual human being, of a direct personal relationship with the ultimate spiritual reality"[24] The God perceived by Einstein, or the ultimate spiritual reality explained by Toynbee, is precisely the Universe Spirit that we are discussing here.

We can further define Universe Spirit in greater detail as follows:

- Universe Spirit is the Naturality-Morality spirit of the universe that reveals itself in humanity as Naturality-Morality in the human stage of the cosmic evolution after advancing from pure natural stages, such as inorganic, microbial, plant, and animal stages. It is a Supernatural Spirit.

- Universe Spirit inspires humanity to self-negate with great willingness through human wisdom and endeavor, thus it advances the Universe evolution to a superhuman stage. It is a Superhuman Spirit.

- Universe Spirit defines intelligence. It brings intelligence into being and gives it self-creative capacity, thus it elevates intelligence continuously to higher levels through its self-creativity. It is a Superintelligence Spirit.

- Universe Sprit defines energy. It gives everything a common energy essence, determines energy in forms of material energy, field energy, and spiritual energy, and makes each of these forms independent but mutually transformable. It is a Superenergy Spirit.

- Universe Spirit makes everything behave as a process. It gives the interaction between all things in space/time the ever-developing nature, thus making the interaction an evolutionary process. It is a Super-evolution Spirit.

- Universe Spirit is the Determine-Counterdeterministic spirit that gives the totality, unity, and orderliness of the universe through determinacy, and manifests the novelty of the universe and its ever-developing and transcending nature through counterdeterminacy. It is a Superdeterministic Spirit.

---

24   Toynbee, Arnold (1976): Mankind and Mother Earth: A Narrative History of the World. New York: Oxford University Press. Page 178, Chapter 25: New Departure in Spiritual Life, C.600-480B.C.

- Universe Spirit defines law. It determines that the development of all things follows definite laws and that the interaction between different laws follows definite laws. It is a Superlaw Spirit.
- Universe Spirit is the spirit that defines science. It is manifested in the incomprehensible universe as mystery to humankind. It enables the mystery to be accessible to human apprehension through acquiring scientific knowledge, and reveals the ultimate reality step by step by drawing mystery and science increasingly together. It is a Superscience Spirit.

To summarize, the Universe Spirit creates the universe, generates everything, and governs all beings. It is a spiritual existence and a divine being; the only and the ultimate reality in the universe; the unification of God, Allah, Buddha, the Tao, and other deities worshipped throughout history.

The history of religion tells us that Judaism comprehended the existence of God through the reflection of the miracles which occurred in Jewish history; Islam came to the realization of Allah through lessons learned from idolatry; Buddhism sensed Buddha through the anatomy of life essence; Taoism perceived the Tao through the quest for natural laws; Confucianism found benevolence through the search for human purpose. These experiences were distinctive and incompatible. However, in today's global age, for any of us with an impartial mind, for any of us with a hope of world peace, we all have a common appreciation of the comprehensiveness, profoundness, and oneness of the Universe Spirit; we all have a common understanding in the determination of the Universe Spirit to guide humanity on the right path, set by its roadmap, from tribal and chiefdom societies, to nation-state and inter-national world, then to state federation, finally to universal brotherhood and a world of spiritual unity.

In a deeper level, religion is the most complex cultural phenomena in human society. First, every religion is based on people's understanding (specially the understanding of the individual religious founder) at a certain stage of history in a higher power or the universe essence. Therefore, religious faith is inevitably conditioned by historical factors, such as societal changes and the stage of human evolution, and conditioned by the personal ability of its founder and successors. Second, religion is deeply rooted in the supremacy, the ultimate, and the oneliness of its believed object. Therefore, once truth and revelation are aggregated into religious teaching, it is long lasting. Third, religious belief has always been a special force that shapes the thinking and governs the souls of its followers. Thus, religious belief fundamentally dominates human society. Because of these factors, it is unfortunate that normal historical limitations in religious teaching, inevitable minor deficiencies in religious scripts, and the personal preferences/emphasis of religious leaders in certain contexts, their expressions in different situations, and the imperfect aspects of their personality have been enlarged, distorted, and deteriorated throughout societal changes and religious expansion. This, thus, leads to misunderstanding, misuse, or even abuse of its original trueness after a period of time. It is not uncommon that some religions/faiths have degenerated into the contrary of their original teaching; some even turn to evil forces that manufacture religious conflicts and faith-based wars.[25] In contrast, anyone with a normal faculties, anyone with common knowledge of modern civilization, anyone with a sense of conscience and justice will have a common appreciation of the mighty force, profound character, and great will of the Universe Spirit that leads humanity towards truth, goodness, beauty, excellence, and happiness, and saves humanity from falsehood, evil, crudity, inferiority, and suffering, throughout five-million-years of human history.

We have described Universe Spirit as the Supernatural, Superhuman, Superintelligence, Superenergy, Superevolution, Superdeterministic, Superlaw, and Superscience Spirit. This implies:

1.   The Universe Spirit reveals the common origin of multiple kingdoms, such as nature, humanity, intelligence, energy, and so on. Therefore, it is the origin and the ultimate of the universe, the first cause and the ultimate destiny of the cosmos.

2.   The Universe Spirit is also the common essence of these kingdoms. Therefore, it is the most fundamental and the holiest part of the universe.

3.   The Universe Spirit, as the common origin and the common essence of these kingdoms, is then the only force that interconnects the cosmos, humankind, and the Creator, communicates between schools of science,

---

25   For example, some religious creeds are still deeply rooted in historical hatred or human primitive instinct that reinforces the ill aspect of humanity, such as the mentality of, "Those who are not part of us must be thinking evil," "Those with whom we share common enemies are our friends," and "Those who have guts prevail in confrontation." This kind of mindset endangers society and creates turmoil from time to time. The more chaotic the society is, the more active and destructive the sentiment is. Some religious teaching still embraces pessimistic cynicism and encourages seeking escape or passively waiting for the next life. Some religions still ignore the progress of human cognition, reject common scientific knowledge, and induce believers to indulge in black magic, manipulate illusions/miracles, and unreasonable occult power. Some faiths have nothing more than a religious shell of institutional formality and a strict rule of worship. In religions like these, many members of various hierarchies have degenerated into parasites of their societies who use religion as a moneymaking tool. Many believers have corrupted into abettors that incite terrorism, inject hatred, advocate violence, and manufacture chaos. This kind of institution has already become the origin of poverty, ignorance, tyranny, violence, brutality, debauchery, and war.

human studies, and theology, unifies the past, present, and future, and reconciles truth, goodness, and beauty.

Coincidentally, the ultimate, the holiness, and the omnipotent nature that we are discussing here is exactly the common characteristic of God, Allah, Buddha, and the Tao. Knowing that, the diversity and historical features of all religions can be easily understood; knowing that, the underlying common pursuit and essence of all faiths will be easily found through Universe Spirit; knowing that, the complementarity and concordance between them will be easily grasped through Universe Spirit. Evidence of religious beliefs and practices can be dated back to 100,000 years ago. In a stricter sense, religion has been accumulated experience for nearly 5000 years. In the last 2000 years, triggered by societal progress and increased interaction, humankind has been taught a tragic lesson by countless religious conflicts and faith-based wars. In today's global world with its current civilization level, we have the responsibility to develop our understanding of the Creator and of religion/faith to a higher level; we have the responsibility to adopt better means to handle inter-religious relations.

In other words, pious religious believers of all faiths, and people in the twenty-first century at large, should not abandon, but rather, assiduously study and thoroughly understand all sacred texts, such as the Bible, the Quran, the Diamond Sutra, the Tao Te Ching. Do not be skeptical, but rather, clearly distinguish the background and context of these sacred scripts and master their true meaning. Do not alter, but rather, firmly believe in, and revere, God, Allah, Buddha, or the Tao. Do not reject, but rather, consciously self-transform to a new theism of the global world. These great sages and their sacred texts reveal the truth of the universe, of the Earth, of humanity, of life, of spirit, and of the Divine in difference languages and from different perspectives. Thus they have truly earned the qualification to educate humanity in the global age. These faiths were the first in history in different parts of the world that definitely and accurately established the supremacy of the Divine with the Universe Spirit as their religious basis and essence from different perspectives and in various ways. Thus, they have been, to date, followed by billions.

In short, the essence of the oneness is the Universe Spirit. The Oneness of All Faiths implies that various gods worshipped throughout history are simply different names given to the same Universe Spirit based on different understandings by the same humanity from different societies. As long as the truth of the Universe Spirit can be revealed, as long as all spiritual beliefs of humanity can be harmonized and unified, it really doesn't matter that this ultimate reality should be labeled in the name of God, or Allah, or Buddha, or the Tao. Fighting for the labeling surely is a misinterpretation of the true teaching of one's faith, a misunderstanding of the original meaning of religious founders, a departure from the Universe Spirit, and a crime in the global age. The concept of the Universe Spirit is an achievement in scientific, human, and theological studies for all humans instead of a religious dogma for some to deal with the others; the belief of the Universe Spirit is a spiritual belief instead of a religious belief or a new religion in any form. Clearly, only in the light of the Universe Spirit concept—a new understanding of spirituality—can every religion be revitalized in the global age; only then can all religions be directed to the right path set by the evolution trend; only then can historical hatred be resolved and peace achieved; only then can people all over the world harmoniously share our human journey. The concept of the Universe Spirit is the new spirituality extracted from the fruit of multiple Middle faiths, particularly from Judaism, Christianity, and Islam.

The Oneness of All Faiths, generally speaking, refers to the God of one religion forming oneness with deity worshipped by any other faith. In a deeper level, it implies all spiritualities share one essence.

We believe that the religious principle based on the essence of the universe, the Universe Spirit manifesting The Oneness of All Faiths, is the concept of spirituality that Middle Civilization has contributed to Global Civilization.

III. Conclusion

What is the message of the above analysis?

It proclaims: the form of human existence has evolved from isolated tribal/national societies for thousands of years. It evolved through the last 300 years, especially the "inter-national" world in twentieth century, and is now rapidly developing into a global world. In this global age, only a universal civilization can fundamentally change the destiny of humanity for the better.

It proclaims: thousands of years of unsuccessful attempts to achieve unity, peace, and harmony are all based on subjective goodwill and are external Band-Aid solutions. In contrast, the oneness concept is based on the intrinsic essence of the matter—a new paradigm that drills commonality from individuality, and, in turn, understands and elevates individuality through commonality.

It proclaims: it is the spirit of The Oneness of All Matter from Western Civilization, the spirit of The Oneness of All Humans from Eastern Civilization, and the spirit of The Oneness of All Faiths from Middle Civilization that constructs Global Civilization for the twenty-first century and the future.

It proclaims: after the significant learning phase that distinguishes humans from the animal kingdom, humanity is now embarking on the profoundest learning phase with Global Civilization as its basic curriculum—promoting civilization by civilized means.

Indeed, philosophical thinking similar to The Oneness of All Matter, The Oneness of All Humans, The Oneness of All Faiths, universal brotherhood, unity of Heaven and Earth, and universal civilization was asserted by sages such as Lao-zi, Zarathustra, Deutero-Isaiah, Socrates, Pythagoras, Confucius, Plato, Gautama, and Jesus as early as 2000 years ago and shortly after by Mohammed. However, the thinking at that time was only an ideal, an extraordinary vision by brilliant individuals, and a vision for the far future rather than for their contemporaries. Although these sages devoted their lifetimes to the endeavor, they achieved little because these objectives were simply too advanced, compared to the historical reality.

Today, we are no longer living in an isolated world of agricultural societies with short-term focus, limited knowledge, and chaotic consciousness. We are already in a world of high integration, in an age of information. It is a time when in-depth knowledge of the microscopic world and broader appreciation of the macroscopic world has been reached, a time when a global society is becoming reality; a time that nurtures Global Civilization, a time that symbolizes the beginning of a new global history; a time that manifests a matured humanity. It is the right time in history because the solid foundation, sufficient objective premise, and appropriate subjective condition are all ready for human endeavor to achieve the oneness of all.

Throughout history, everyone pursued truth, goodness, and beauty. The Oneness of All Matter is the truth in the twenty-first century; The Oneness of All Humans is goodness in the twenty-first century, and The Oneness of All Faith is beauty in twenty-first century.

Throughout the world, everyone emphasizes knowledge, compassion, and meaningfulness. The Oneness of All Matter is the knowledge in the global world; The Oneness of All Humans is the compassion in the global world, and The Oneness of All Faiths is the meaningfulness in the global world.

Throughout history, everyone strove for spatial advantage, human harmony, and temporal opportunity. Spatial advantage is to be produced through the principle of The Oneness of All Matter; human harmony is to be achieved through the principle of The Oneness of All Humans; temporal opportunity emerges through the principle of The Oneness of All Faiths.

Throughout the world, everyone calls for liberty, equality, and benevolence. Only The Oneness of All Matter can lead to true liberty; only The Oneness of All Humans can lead to true equality; only The Oneness of All Faiths can lead to true benevolence.

Grounding The Oneness of All Matter—All things have the same Determine-Counterdeterminacy thus form the oneness of all.

Promoting The Oneness of All Humans—All people have the same Naturality-Morality thus must be mutually supportive in a universal brotherhood.

Achieving The Oneness of all Faiths—spirituality has the same essence of the Universe Spirit, thus believers of all faiths should be in a harmonious human journey together.[26]

---

26   We can discuss this further: all things in the universe, humanity, and spirituality share one essence thus form oneness. This oneness has three underlying implications: first, the oneness of all things, humanity, and spirituality makes the universe an organic whole; second, the oneness of humans' body, mind, and spirit makes the existence of human life; third, the oneness of the organic cosmos and the human life existence makes the trinity of cosmos/earth/human. The interconnectedness of the trinity is the origin of telepathic communication between humanity and heaven (or God) that occurs throughout history, the reason of the emergence of numerous prophets throughout history. Therefore, the oneness exists in all matter, all humans, and all Divines, as well as in naturality, humanity, and divinity.

Furthermore, as we discussed earlier, Determine-Counterdeterminacy is the cause of universe creation, its structural principle, and law of evolution, so it is the fundamental essence in the universe and the cosmic soul. If Determine-Counterdeterminacy is the fundamental spirit in the universe, the soul of the cosmos, it is then the ultimate spiritual reality. The Universe Spirit creates the reaction of the physical world, the sensation of plant life, the awareness of animal life, and the consciousness of human life. It is possible to apprehend the ultimate spirit only by thinking outside the fixed human paradigms and breaking common human assumption in conceptions like animal consciousness and human spirit.

As the ultimate spiritual reality of the universe, Determine-Counterdeterminacy has properties of both definite and infinite aspects. Its definite aspect includes five levels, from low to high, namely (1) reactive-knowing (such as physical or chemical reactions), (2) sensory-knowing (such as the sensory perception of biological life), (3) cognitive-knowing (such as the mind power and cognitive ability of animal life), (4) self-knowing (such as the self-awareness and the reflective ability of human life), and (5) foreknowing (such as the foreseeing ability of prophethood, and the Extrasensory Perception ability of some who are aware of events before their actual happening). Its infinite aspect also has five levels, from low to high, namely (1) direct-knowing (transcending logicalness), (2) transcendental-knowing (transcending provableness), (3) original-knowing (transcending objectiveness), (4) ever-knowing (timelessness and eternality), and (5) all-knowing (omniscient, omnipotent, and omnipresent).

Prior to universe time, numerous preuniverse elements (initial material energy) interplayed in chaos through the preuniverse field (primordial field energy). The overall outcome of this interplay gradually approached—maybe "searched for" is more appropri-

This is the conclusion of the Declaration of Global Civilization.

---

ate—a kind of structure. Eventually the Determine-Counterdeterministic structure was chosen and set forth because only Determine-Counterdeterministic interaction is able to develop the chaos, symmetry, and reversibility of the preuniverse into orderliness, asymmetry, and irreversibility, and only Determine-Counterdeterministic interaction is able to achieve cosmic stableness in the developing process in the dimension of time. The setting of the Determine-Counterdeterministic model indicates that the interpenetrated Determine-Counterdeterministic interaction has reached a critical point, a breakthrough point that is defined by the interaction. More profoundly, this critical point symbolizes the formation of the spiritual energy with self-reflective, self-adjusting, self-creative, and self-transcending nature. The most fundamental issue in Cosmology is to reveal the spiritual aspect of the initial universe and its later stages because only spiritual energy has the ability to define its structure, set the objective of its development, and self-adjust to achieve the objective.

At this point, a new energy system—the universe—was created by the integration of material energy, field energy, and spiritual energy with spiritual energy as its leading force and Determine-Counterdeterminacy as its essence. It is the Universe Spirit that integrated these three forms of energy and unified them into a self-constructive, self-evolutionary whole. It is Determine-Counterdeterminacy that brought the Universe Spirit into being and manifested its self-constructive and self-evolutionary essence. Determine-Counterdeterminacy sets everything in the web of interconnectedness, hence transforms and reinforces everything as energy intermediate being; it turns the cosmos into a system of energy, hence provides and elevates the intelligence and vitality of the universe; it integrates material energy, field energy, and spiritual energy into an organic whole hence provides and enhances its orderliness and direction of evolution; it executes the orderly regularity in all planes of the universe and controls the interplay between them. This is the magnificent magic of the Universe Spirit. It is the profoundest significance of the Universe Spirit. It is the magic and significance of God. Renowned Austrian astrophysicist Erich Jantsch stated, "God is not the Creator, rather, He is the Mind of the universe." In fact, a revision of this quote makes more sense: God is the Creator, because He is the Mind of the universe.

Indeed, the Universe Spirit with Determine-Counterdeterminacy as its essence has properties of both the definite and infinite aspects, namely reactive-knowing, sensory-knowing, cognitive-knowing, self-knowing, foreknowing, direct-knowing, transcendental-knowing, self-knowing, ever-knowing, and all-knowing. It, therefore, has the power to reveal itself as the cosmic model with Determine-Counterdeterminacy as its basic nature; the power to maintain the cosmic orderliness with Determine-Counterdeterminacy as its fundamental regularity, and the power to follow the cosmic evolution process preprogrammed by Determine-Counterdeterminacy. Humankind, the special species on earth with Naturality-Morality, is a new cosmic form created at the critical point after a prolonged period of nurturing by the cosmos. In this sense, the concept of Universe-Spirit is about the essence of the universe. Determine-Counterdeterminism is about the essence of the Universe Spirit; and the concept of Naturality-Morality is about how the Universe Spirit creates humanity, provides it with Naturality-Mortality, and establishes the unity of Human Nature and Race Nature as the model of human existence. In other words, the Universe acquires its spirit by choosing Determine-Counterdeterminacy; humanity acquires the nature of Naturality-Morality from the Universe Spirit; Determine-Counterdeterminacy defines itself through Universe-Spirit and Naturality-Morality. Hence, these three parties—Determine-Counterdeterminacy, Naturality-Morality, and the Universe-Spirit—also share one essence and form oneness.

The appreciation of the oneness will lead us to a profound realization: (1) the origin of the universe is the result of the single point effect coupled by Deterministic and Counterdeterministic elements of the Preuniverse after a prolonged period of mutual attraction and fine-tuning (examples of similar single point effects are: the point of divergence in theory of dissipative structures, the point of differentiation in life science, the enlightening point of human's consciousness and conscience), (2) the order of the universe is the perfect cosmic condition in all dimensions, a critical state determined by multiple parameters, set forth by the interpenetrating and mutual supporting Deterministic and Counterdeterministic actions of the universe (A similar critical state is the origin of annual rings on a woody plant, and the origin of an animal's life span), (3) the development of the universe is a process preprogrammed by Determine-Counterdeterministic spirit, towards its destiny step by step (examples of a similar preprogrammed process are: the trend of biological evolution from low to high levels, personal fate of human beings, the sequence of human cognition development from sensing, knowing, to reasoning and enlightening), (4) the destiny of the universe is an orderly dynamic process, moving step by step towards its ultimate destination, in which the universe continuously advances to higher structural levels and continuously creates novelty through Determine-Counterdeterministic interactions but within the critical state defined by Determine-Counterdeterminacy, (5) the creation of humanity is the cosmic response to its evolutionary request in accordance with the Universe Spirit when evolution reaches a stage that only a self-creative power of a body-mind being can lead the evolution to the next level. Therefore, the true purpose of human life is contributing to the cosmic evolutionary dynamic as a new element of biological intelligence, rather than a competing survival and satisfaction of personal desire that people took for granted throughout history.

We can see from the above analysis that Determine-Counterdeterminacy, Naturality-Morality, and the Universe-Spirit share one essence and thus form oneness. Determine-Counterdeterminacy manifests The Oneness of All Matter; Naturality-Morality manifests The Oneness of All Humans; Universe-Spirit manifests The Oneness of All Faiths. Therefore, these three onenesses share one essence and form a greater oneness. The relation of the three onenesses could be illustrated more clearly by an analogy with that of the Holy Trinity in Christianity: Determine-Counterdeterminacy is the Holy Spirit, Universe-Spirit is God, the Father, and Naturality-Morality is God, the Son. The trinity here also implies the three onenesses are one and the essence of this oneness is Determine-Counterdeterminacy. In other words, Determine-Counterdeterminacy determines the Universe Spirit, and the Universe Spirit determines Naturality-Mortality. The latter ones counterdetermine the former ones, respectively.

This declaration attempts to address civilization issues theoretically. Detailed analysis in topics such as the purpose of humanity, the spirit of the universe, the nature of the Divine, and the relation of these three onenesses is not presented. These important topics deserve separate discussions.

The Original Version of The Declaration of Global Civilization
in Chinese

全球文明宣言

全球文明第一届世界大会通过

2001·7·悉尼

目录

全球文明宣言[1]

（全球文明第一届世界大会通过）

由全球文明推进组织发起和主办，我们来自37个国家的科学界、宗教界、政界、哲学界、文学艺术界、实业界的50位正式代表和30位特邀嘉宾，于2001年7月16—18日在澳大利亚悉尼市希尔顿饭店，召开了"全球文明第一届世界大会"。大会以45票赞成、一票基本赞成、两票弃权、一票缺席、一票反对，通过了这部关系到人类未来命运的《全球文明宣言》。**这也是人类历史上面向全人类的第一部理论性宣言。**

一. 总 论

今年，2001年，这是新世纪的元年，也是新千年的元年。人类经过自产生以来的漫长进化，正在进入一个堪与"猴子变人"相媲美的转轨期。这个转轨期有两个标志：一是人类正在从千百年来的生产方式、社会制度、意识形态上的进步，转向"文明"这一人类生存最深层面的进步；二是人类正在从千百年来的部落世界、国家世界、国家间世界转向"全球世界"这一活动范围最为广阔的世界。

因此，在文明问题占主导地位的21世纪，只有从文明问题入手，才能真正解决世界的难题；在迅速形成全球世界的21世纪，只有确立一种"全球文明"，才能从根本上改变人类的命运。

1　《全球文明宣言》第一稿于1999年7月—12月在美国、俄罗斯、中国、英国、德国、荷兰、伊朗、新加坡、罗马尼亚等国家的有关学者中讨论。

第二稿于2000年1月—12月向世界各国有关人士征求意见，此间得到了97个国家包括国家元首、宗教领袖、诺贝尔奖获得者在内的各界人士的关注、支持和修改意见。

第三稿提交2001年7月16—18日召开的"全球文明第一届世界大会"讨论并通过。

本宣言的第一稿、第二稿、大会讨论稿和读者面前的这份正式文本，均由中国学者、全球文明推进组织主席章韶华创作和修订。

本宣言的中文文本为标准文本。

我们不能停留于"21世纪将是文明问题占主导地位的世纪"这种认识，这已是不争的事实；不能满足于泛泛谈论促进世界文明、地球文明、人类文明，这种作法于事无补；也不能致力于寻找逃避、抑或迎接文明冲突的药方，这是让人们饮鸩止渴。

今天，最需要的是让人类了解，全球时代的人类究竟需要什么样的文明；最重要的是让人类懂得，文明冲突的真正根源就在现有的文明本身。这也就是说，从理论上解决全球时代必然产生的文明冲突，已经成为实际地解决文明冲突的先决条件。因此，顺应全球时代，对"文明"进行一次彻底的理论剖析，使人类从此告别"总是用非文明、反文明的方式推进文明"的历史，正是创作、讨论并通过这部宣言的目的。

1.　　全球文明的提出和意义

20世纪下半叶，这是人类历史上发生的第一次全球性的、来自文明的大混乱时期。

在绝大多数地区和国家，文明的先决条件——法律、秩序和信仰，走到了崩溃的边沿；文明的内在活力——信任、理想和自信，几乎降到了极限。深到家庭理念、社会公德，大至政府功能、意识形态，都在直线下滑；而犯罪、贩毒、恐怖的跨国活动，国家、民族、宗教之间的暴力冲撞，却在直线上升。许多国家、特别是大国强国、尤其是文明核心国，以文明认同为参照系的国际阵营重组、军事范围编程、特别是核力量的部局，已经从谨小慎微的暗中交易变成光天化日之下的歃血为盟。在公众那里、特别是青年学生中、尤其在知识分子精英中，由融入全球化与坚持本土化的矛盾引起的种族主义情绪、民族主义情绪、国家主义情绪，抑或反国家情绪、反民族情绪、反政府情绪，正像肆虐的洪水，先是冲破了理智的闸门，接着又冲决了良知的堤坝……

总之，在世界范围内，人类文明的许多方面正在让位于有奶就是娘的婴儿思维、唯我独尊的疯子心态、弱肉强食的动物法则。新千年的开始正在重现旧千年开始时的许多特征，新世纪初的人类正在拉开上世纪初的悲剧序幕。有人慨然："一个全球的'黑暗时代'也许正在降临人类"[2]。

认真分析全球混乱的原因是重要的。

20世纪前半叶连续两次世界大战，一方面把几乎所有民族推上了世界舞台，一方面战争的巨大消耗和空前灾难迫使人类进入了相对持久的战后和平期，亦即人们常说的"冷战时期"。战争的后遗症，使各国政府很自然地把精力集中到了发展军事技术上。世界性的军事技术创新诱发了科学技术的腾飞，而相对持久的和平则为此提供了极为有利的环境。科技现代化引发了经济全球化，经济全球化反过来刺激着科技现代化。于是，以经济全球化和科技现代化的相互催化为特色的时代风暴，加剧了以美国为首的资本主义阵营、以苏联为首的社会主义阵营、众多不结盟国家这三者之间政治上军事上的剑拔弩张。反过来，这三大国际势力的明争暗斗，又刺激着全球化和现代化。然而，真正深层面的问题却是，全球化现代化中的各个民族，正在把彼此不同的传统观念、文化模式、宗教信仰等文明精神，以"现代"的速度悄悄带进了"全球"这同一个角斗场。由于任何民族对于自己的文明模式有着深入骨髓的自洽性和不由自主的认同感，所以，随着全球化、现代化的深入，本土文明之间似乎注定要进行一场激烈决斗、甚至集体搏斗。

人类当然会逃避这场后果难料的文明冲突。回头看，"二战"结束不久，在排山倒海的全球化、现代化中，面对不同文化、不同价值、不同信仰越来越频繁的磨擦，各民族在如何对待文明冲撞问题上采取了相同的对策，即都选择了返回传统、回归民族、回到本土这条回头路。从偏远部落到繁华都市，从年轻学生到科学精英，从普通百姓到国家元首，每个民族、每种文化、每个宗教、甚至许多百姓，都在疾声发问："我们是谁？""我们的祖先是谁？""他们是谁？""他们要把我们引向哪里？"这些追问，一方面导致了欧盟、阿盟、非盟等以文明认同为标准的国际联盟的匆匆建立，另一方面使得旧的殖民体系、传统国际联盟、特别是刚刚建立的社会主义阵营等这些"跨文明国际阵

2 《文明冲突与世界秩序重建》［美］塞缪尔·亨廷顿著，中译本，ISBN-7-5011-3872-9，第372页。

营"的迅速解体。

社会主义大家庭、特别是其轴心苏－东体系的分崩离析，引发了突然失去宿敌也再没了配作对手的、以美国为先导的西方体系的迅速外投。西方文明，特别是美国文明，尤其是美国人的价值观、人生观、信仰观等，借助高新科技的发散、经济市场的开拓、军事范围的扩张，惊醒了全世界几乎所有处于长期冬眠中的本土文明。于是，各本土文明尚未来得及弄清事情的原由，便蜂拥而上、鸣鼓应战。这种局面，又反过来使"挑战者"始料未及，乱了方寸。这就使得这场不同文明间集体决斗的所有参与者，既缺乏准备又缺少裁判，既充满自尊又缺乏自信。我们可以清晰地看到，这场文明混乱中的各方有一个共同的特点，那就是：它们仍在按照殖民习惯、强权思维、战争意识等旧的方式来处理"全球世界"中的矛盾、来解决文化上宗教上的磨擦，都在像分切蛋糕一样从本国利益、本族传统、本土文化出发来参与全球化和现代化。简言之，各个民族一方面都在极力让自己全球化、现代化，一方面又在拼命捍卫本土文明的理念。

可见，这是一个缺乏理论准备、政治准备和心理准备却又完全符合事物发展逻辑的全球化现代化阶段，是一个充满被动性、盲目性和自发性的本土文明汇合期。这就不可避免地形成了十分荒诞的现象：国家间本来早已过去的历史恩怨、民族间本来合理的历史差异、文化中本来正常的历史局限，却因全球性会合、现代性交往，变成了国家间口蜜腹剑、民族间尔虞我诈、宗教上唯我独尊、文化上水火不容的非文明关系。

不同文明之间的非文明交往必然导致反文明的结局，这就是，各个民族为了捍卫本土的文明精神，不得不践踏经过几千年甚至上万年的摸索方才确立的"作为人类"的最基本的文明；虽然融入了全球化、步入了现代化，却在文明层面上远离了全球社会、现代精神。甚至可以这样说，各本土文明似乎都在丧失理智地强化本文明的弱点、背离本文明的优点，从而也诱发了它文明的弱点、缩小了它文明的优点。可惜的是，各本土文明中的这些优点，正是各民族经过痛苦而漫长的摸索方才确立的优秀文明成果——那些既具有人类普适性、又具有永恒价值的文明精神。回顾"二战"之后国际上的许多重大事件，如儿童游戏似的美苏军备竞赛、毫无道理的朝鲜战争、毫无章法的越南战争、莫名其妙的苏联入驻阿富汗、因小失大的两伊战争、伊拉克疯了似的占领科威特、一群疯子教训一个疯子的海湾战争、背离时代潮流的北约东扩等等，以及国家内部发生的许多重大事件，如卢旺达种族大屠杀、伊拉克政府对库尔德人的种族大屠杀、斯雷布雷尼察种族大屠杀、中国文化大革命、阿富汗塔里班大事变等等，都可以清楚地发现这一点。然而，真正让人担忧的是，这类丧失理智的闹剧，这类泯灭良知的悲剧，刚刚开始[3]。

到底谁之罪？全都无罪；究竟谁之错？谁也没错。比如上面的每个事件，都有它充足的理由，每一个理由又都合乎本文明的"章法"。如果硬要追查，只能是罪在规律、错在时代。问题在于，规律和时代从来都是引领人类前进的两位"天使"，它们从不犯罪、从无差错。人类在思索着，追问着，求证着。一个谜语，可以有各种各样的推论，却只有一个谜底。而这个谜语的谜底就是，由各本土文明的全球汇合引起的全球混乱，正在唤醒各国对包括本文明在内的所有界域文明那种局限性、偏执性、陈旧性、片面性的强烈不满和痛苦反思。质言之，以不同文明

3　我们还可以作进一步的分析。

经济全球化起因于科技的现代化，科技现代化来自西方文明的独特素质。但是，人性追求、个性实现是文明的深层部分，文化制约、传统作用是文明的中层部分，而经济活动、科技创新只是文明的外层形态。所以，全球化不是殖民化，现代化也不等于西化。强国大国可以占领弱小国家，可以统治弱小民族，却不能控制它们的信念和灵魂。这样，当着以美国文明为先导的西方文明按照文明演进的正常逻辑，伴随着国际市场的拓展、高新科技的传播，把自己的价值观念、人权观念、宗教观念也全球化的时候，便爆发了各本土文明之间深层面的混战。面对这种情况，先是非西方的民族——最后也迫使西方的民族，不得不迅速调整思路使自己的文明迅速归位，那些处于文明边缘和缝隙的民族则在仓促地选择自己的文明归属。

回顾20世纪后半叶，特别是20世纪的后二十年，世界各民族为了应付来势汹汹的全球化和现代化，都在慌慌张张地寻找或缩回能够保护自己的"文明之壳"。然而，全球化、现代化虽然来源于西方，却不仅仅适宜于西方，相反，它不仅是人类进步的必然结果，而且可以造福于整个人类。这决定了全球化现代化的进程，既不可能停止，又不可能转向，更不可能回头。这就使得曾经通行了几千年的本土文明之壳、区域文明之壳，已经不再是安全的巢穴。更为严重的是，全球化浪潮与本土性文明、现代化精神与传统性文化的这些强烈反差、猛烈冲撞，还引发了各本土文明内部的剧烈动荡、深层扭变。

间冲突为特色的全球混乱，其实是在预示着人类文明将进入一个全新的阶段，一个以"全球文明"为文明特征的人类新文明阶段。

人是文明的被塑者，也是文明的改塑者，更是文明的创新者。面对文明冲突可能引发的新一轮的地区战争和世界大战、新形式的种族灭绝和宗教吞并，人类理所当然地要审查所有本土文明中那些导致全球混乱的有害元素和陈腐逻辑。

果然如此，纵观今日世界，我们发现，在全球混乱的深层，一种预示着人类希望的"全球文明精神"，正在许多国家以各自的方式悄悄成长起来。例如，试图让不同文明和睦相处的澳大利亚多元文化政策，尝试把西方价值与东方价值结合在一起的新加坡道路，逐渐把人权提升为国家第一权力的美国精神，主动敞开本文明之门的伊朗文明对话之路，以主张应天顺势与提倡世界大同为特点的道－儒精神在中国的复兴，以平等心态积极融入欧亚大陆体系的俄罗斯新思维，把新世纪元年定为"各文明间对话年"的联合国决议，如此等等。尽管这些努力具有明显的探索性质，但其内在趋势却是在试图克服本族文明的狭隘，却是在朝向全球文明的目标。

按照这种分析，风靡全球的文明冲突论、文化本土论、文化寻根论，虽然基于活生生的现实，却是一条倒退之路；与之相对立的文明对话论、文化共处论、文化融合论，虽然表达了当代人们的善意，却又缺乏客观上的基础。因为，在今天的国家框架中，在本土文明圈子里，在现有的文明理念下，既不可能缓解文明间深层的冲突，也不可能展开文明间真正的对话；因为，国家中心思维、本土文明理念、原教旨情结，本身就是文明冲突的根源、文明对话的障碍；因为，任何本土文明，只能得心应手地解决本土之内的问题，却不可能解决"文明之间"的问题；因为，本土文明之间的矛盾必须采用与之相应的方法，一种既体现本土文明共性、又高于本土文明境界的方法，而这种方法正是"全球文明"的方法[4]。

　　4　比方说，面对20世纪末叶的无序、混乱和失控，各国的政治家、宗教家、学者和公众，几乎是同时呼吁：尽快建立新的世界政治经济秩序。然而，要想建立大多数国家都能认同的世界秩序，首先就要确立一种普适于全人类的文明精神——全球文明精神。

总之，延续了五千多年的本土文明模式，持续了三百多年的文明扩张习惯，特别是自"二战"结束以来积蓄了半个多世纪的利益争端、政治僵持、军事冷战、文化渗透、宗教磨擦，一个共同的和根本的原因，就是在近万年所形成的人类文明体系中，缺少一种"跨本土跨区域的即面向全世界、体现人类性的文明精神"——"全球文明精神"。这样，历史给21世纪只剩下了唯一一条通向光明的道路，这就是：**以全球化、现代化为立足点，以人类的相同本性、共同福祉为参照系，在提取各本土文明优良元素的基础上，构筑一种超越了本土文明的、适应全球时代和现代认识的、具有全球性现代性的文明——全球文明**[5]。

显然，只有借助全球文明这一本土文明的普照光和公约数，才能显现出不同文明的共性部分，暴露出本土文明的优劣元素，寻找到不同文明交往的安全通道，摸索出提升本土文明的正确途径。这，就是全球文明的基本意义。

2. 全球文明的含义和理念

文明，有广义和狭义之分。狭义的文明与愚昧、野蛮、原始相对立，这也是文明的绝对性含义；广义的文明则是指人类的生存模式及其发展——作为某种生存方式，昨天是文明的，今天就可能是非文明的了，所以，这又是文明的相对性含义。

在全球时代到来之前，文明一直是指一定数量的不同人类群体内共同的生存模式。所以，迄今为止所有的文明，部落文明、民族文明、国家文明等本土文明，欧洲文明、非洲文明、东方文明、西方文明等区域文明，在本质上都属于"界域文明"。界域文明是文明的、自治的，又

---

5 我们选择"全球文明"概念而不用"人类文明"，是因为后者只是一个日常用语，比如，曾存的现存的任何一种文明都属于人类文明。与之相反，"全球文明"既不同于任何既有的文明模式，又表达了人们适时地从人类整体角度把握文明、推进文明的愿望。我们也没有采用"世界文明"概念，这是因为"世界"在历史上和现实中一直都是一个含义极不确定、使用甚为混乱的概念，世界文明并不能准确表达我们所说的全球文明的含义，而全球文明则从更深的层面表达了"世界文明"表述文明时所指征的意思。

是局部的、排它的。本来是一种文明，却又本能地或排斥、或吞并、或同化其它文明，从而使自己反倒显现出非文明、反文明的弱点，这是所有界域文明的共同特征和主要弊端。

与之不同，全球文明精神则以推进全世界各民族的文明为明确目的，它揭示的是各民族作为同一个人类的不同群体都必然具有、都必须具备的文明——共性文明。

所以，从一般意义上讲，全球文明有两个意思：一个是"全球的文明"，即启发和帮助各本土文明找到一条适合全球生存的道路、用以实现本土文明的升次，这是一般意义上的全球文明，这时它面对的是各本土文明的个性；另一个是"全球性文明"，即为全球化现代化时代的人们确立一种普适于全体人类的、体现了现代精神的文明模式，这是严格意义上的全球文明，这时它体现的是各本土文明的共性[6]。推进"全球的文明"是目的，采用"全球性文明"是方法，两者相互确证、互相补益、是二而一。只有抱着这样的目的、采用这样的方法，才称得上"用文明的方式推进文明"。

如果把全球文明的含义再细化一些，它包括三个方面：

第一，从形式上讲，全球文明是人性文明与类性文明的统一。人类，一般说来，是"人"属性与"类"属性的统一。从这个意义上看，全球文明既是一个独立概念，又是一个整体概念。

作为独立概念，全球文明侧重于从人科、人种、人属即"人"的角度，亦即生物学、人类学的角度来界定文明。它的意义在于，只有用"人文明"的理念，即用"不同界域文明中的人们同属于人"的理念，才能挖掘出各界域文明中的共性。

作为整体概念，全球文明侧重于从"人类是由全部个体、所有群体整合而成的整体"的角度即"类"的角度，亦即社会学、文化学的角度来界定文明。它的意义在于，只有用"人类本质上是一个有机整体"这

6　所以，全球文明并不排斥本土文明，恰恰相反，它的产生是对"尊重本土文明，保护本土文明"呼声的理性回应。不仅如此，它还超越了本土文明，这使它具有了这样一种力量：只有这种全球文明才能够居高临下、提纲挈领，给全球化时代的各本土文明，提供现代生存的方向、化解文明冲突的方法，特别是为避免随时都可能爆发的文明间的战争，提供最后一道、也是最坚固的一道保险层。

种"类文明"的理念,即用"人类既有作为特定物种的人性,更有社会的文化的道德的属性即类性"的理念,才能提升各界域文明的层次[7]。

一只脚立于"人人同祖"之基,一只脚立于"人类一体"之基,这便是全球文明的根基所在。

第二,从内容上讲,全球文明是个体文明与全体文明的统一。人类,严格说来,是所有个体与人类全体的统一。从这个意义上看,全球文明既是一个单体概念,又是一个集体概念。

作为单体概念,全球文明侧重于从个体的角度界定文明。它的意义在于,只有用"真正的文明一定是植根于每个人的文明"这种"人权文明"的理念,才能判定文明素质的优劣。

作为集体概念,全球文明侧重于从全体的角度界定文明。它的意义在于,只有用"真正的文明一定是立足于全人类的文明"这种"类权文明"的理念,才能判定文明境界的高低[8]。

一只手把个体引入全体的境界,一只手把全体的能力特化为个体的素质,这正是全球文明的目的所在。

第三,从性质上讲,全球文明是元文明与大文明的统一。人类,全面说来,还是人类生性与人类生境的统一。从这个意义上讲,全球文明既是一个特指概念,又是一个泛指概念。

作为特指概念,全球文明侧重于从"人类生性"的角度界定文明。文明,是一个严整的人类生存系统,从纵向上讲,可以分为三个层次:

---

7 人文明与类文明是统一的。任何不尊重人的物质需要、肉体本能、自然环境即"种本性"的文明,都不可能是好的文明;任何放任"种本性"而无视人的社会本性、文化需要、情感满足即"类本性"的文明,也不可能是好的文明。同样,任何不尊重人的生而平等、生性自由、人生权力即"种规定"的文明,都不可能是好的文明;任何放任"种规定"而无视人的社会责任、道德修养、人格培植即"类规定"的文明,也不可能是好的文明。

8 个体文明与全体文明也是内在统一的。只要是个体最基本的需求,一定也是全体所需要的;只有合乎全体人类的,才是真正符合每个个人的;个体发展的道路,总是伸向全体;全体进化的方向,总是指向个体。这是人类、个人的真正秘密,也是任何文明、文化的真正秘密。从这一点看,人类历史上顺序经历的氏族文明、部落文明、宗族文明、民族文明、国家文明、区域文明等,都是个体人类化、人类个体化这一人类文明总进程的必然过渡、中介环节。

政治、经济、社会的"体制"是文明的表层，习俗、观念、信仰等"文化"是文明的中层，人类对自己的人性、类性、群体特性、个体个性等"人类本性"方面的理解和追求是文明的深层。任何一种文明，都是它的人们的生存秩序、文化模式、人性意识有机统一的整体。这也就是说，迄今为止的区域文明、国家文明、民族文明，是侧重于从体制上反映文明的表层文明；习俗文明、宗教文明、科技文明，是侧重于从文化上反映文明的中层文明；而全球文明则是侧重于从对人类多重属性的理解和追求上来揭示文明的深层文明。所谓深层文明，严格说来，也就是"元文明"。"元"，顾名思义，是首要、本原、基础的意思。人类首要、本原、基础的东西是什么？是人的人性和类性。而人类的人性和类性的统一，即是人类的生性——人类的生命本性及其生存本性。所以，元文明也就是关于人类生性的文明。显然，这种元文明是人类文明体系中最根本、最普通、最普适的文明理念，也是诸如政治文明、物质文明、科技文明、道德文明、信仰文明等得以滋生的土壤。

　　作为泛指概念，全球文明侧重于从"人类生境"的角度界定文明。文明，还是一种界面清晰的作用范围，所以，从横向上讲，它又分为范围大小不同的三个文明圈：一是界域文明圈，如部落文明、中华文明、印度文明、东方文明、西方文明等，这是一种小文明；二是全域文明圈即全人类的文明、全世界的文明，这是一种中文明。这两种都属于人类自身的文明。除此之外，还有一种作为人类文明发生原因、先决条件和作用对象并将小文明和中文明包括其中的"生境文明圈"，也就是人们常说的包括环境文明、地外文明、星际文明、地球生物圈文明、人类之前地球上可能出现过的文明等等在内的与人类相关的文明圈。其实，全球文明中"全球"与"文明"的整合本身就内含了与周围环境的关系，从而使"全球"必然是一个与外互为、向外开放即"文明"的系统。所以，从这个意义上讲，全球文明又是一种生境文明。与中、小文明相比，它显然又是一种"大文明"。大文明包容着、提升着中文明、小文明，中文明、小文明滋养着、驱动着大文明。所以，这种大文明是人类文明体系中最深厚、最开阔、最高级的文明理念，也是诸如社区文明、民族文明、国家文明、区域文明、人类文明等得以存在的基础和成长的土壤[9]。

一方面让人类的生境生性化，一方面让人类的生性生境化，这才是全球文明的真义所在。……

如果这样来解释全球文明，那么，它好像是人类文明体系中常识性的、一般性的、可以忽略的部分。其实，刚好相反，在我们看来，正是这种全球文明，构成了21世纪人类文明体系中最丰富、最根本、最光辉的部分。例如，全球文明系统应当包括：以世界联合国会、世界联合政府、世界联合司法会为标志的人类新政治体系，以世界宪法、世界联军法、世界政党法、世界公民法、国家法、国家边境法、国家元首法、国家立法法等法律为主体的人类新法律体系，以立足全球生态、尊重自然生态、发展科学生态、着眼未来生态为框架的人类新生态体系，以缩小贫富差距、建立公正机制、调整资源归属、协调人口密度为原则的人类新经济体系，以整合各大宗教相似而又合理的即具有人类普适性的教义、教理、教规为特色的人类新宗教体系，以生存安全化、生活人性化为明确目的和检验标准的人类新科技体系，以公民自由、国家自主、世界统一、天人互塑为主要内容的人类新道德体系，以本土文化与全球文化、生性文化与生境文化、传统文化与现代文化的良性互动为特征的人类新文化体系，如此等等。可见，"全球文明……是更高层次的道德、宗教、知识、艺术、哲学、技术、物质福祉等等的混合体[10]。"

既然如此，那么，对于今天的和今后的政治领袖、宗教领袖、商界领袖、学界领袖来说，21世纪真正需要你们的，并不是所谓驾驭文明冲突的智慧、容忍不同文明的气度、学习其它文明的胸襟、遏制反文明行为的勇气，而是转变自己的文明观念、提升自己的文明境界，即真正从字母、发音和拼写学起，尽快学会"全球文明"这门新文明课程。

9　元文明与大文明也是统一的。元文明是全球文明的"全息胚"，大文明是全球文明的"特化系"。凡是深层存在的，一定是广泛适用的；任何广泛性的东西，也一定是深层次的东西。回顾人类文明史，是否体现元文明与大文明的统一，乃是判断文明优劣、衡量文明高低、决定文明久短的根本标准。

10　《文明冲突与世界秩序重建》［美］塞缪尔·亨廷顿著，中译本，ISBN-7-5011-3872-9，第370页。

进而言之，领袖是公众按照自己意愿选举出来的代表人物，所以，在21世纪的所有问题中，最迫切的问题是教育人类，即让人类用全球文明精神自己教育自己、让民众和领袖互相教育。在人类诞生至今的五百万年间，出现过两次伟大的人类学习期。第一次是刚刚脱离动物界时面对的那次学习期，那一次是学习直立行走，学习制造和使用工具，学习劳动，学习用火，学习语言，学习结社，学习文明，总之是学习用人类之"人"的方式即"人科生物"的方式面对世界；第二次是生活在21世纪的人类——我们——遇到的这次学习期，这一次是学习人人平等，学习世界和平，学习人类公义，学习宇宙大义，学习认识人自己，学习自己管理自己，学习做世界公民，学习做地球之子，学习用文明的方式推进文明，总之是学习用人类之"类"的方式即"类体生物"的方式面对世界。所以，如果说，第一次学习期是学习如何在本土范围内、群体条件下文明的生活，那么，第二次学习期则是学习如何在全球范围内、类体条件下文明的生活。可见，第二次学习期的根本特点和基础课程，就是全球文明[11]。

那么，全球文明这门课程为我们提出了哪些新的课题呢？

第一，现存的种种本土文明，既有各自的个性，更有任何本土文明同属人类文明的共性。并且，只有用文明的这种共性，才能理解和优化本土文明的个性，才能化解和根除本土文明间的冲突，也只有采取这种方法才是"用文明的方式推进文明"。因此，**任何非文明、反文明方法都不可能推进严格意义上的文明。这是人类近万年文明史提供的"第一经验"。**

第二，以往的文明都是在部落中心时代、国家中心时代、区域中心时代形成的，所以，不同文明之间有差别、有争论完全是正常现象，但是，今天的人们无论以何种理由把差别、争论引向冲突、战争，或者以经济制裁、政治胁迫、军事打击进行文化渗透和文明输出，都是直接反

---

11 是的，人类对文明的正确认识来得太迟了。生而为人、身为人类，近万年的文明史过去了，可惜，文明的巨大能量、人类的创造能力，千百年来一直被严格圈禁在国家框架、教派领地、民族传统等一个个贫瘠而狭窄的圈子里，以至于到了最近10多年人们才发现，在我们人类生存的这个地球上，竟然还存在一种叫做"全球文明"的东西。

文明的。因此，**把不同文明间或同一文明内不同派别间的争执，严格限制在避免武装冲突的范围以内，这是21世纪的"第一原则"。**

第三，部落中心时代，部落利益高于一切；国家中心时代，国家利益高于一切；在人类日趋一体化的21世纪，只有诸如地球外环境、地球生态、人类资源、世界和平、人生权利等人类整体的利益才是每个地区、每个国家、每个教徒、每个公民的根本利益。因此，**全人类的利益是高于其它利益的"第一利益"。**

第四，人是宇宙的精品，不是宇宙的圣者，更不是宇宙的灵魂；人是地球之子，不是众生之主，更不是地球之王；人是类居生物，不是群居生物，更不是独居生物；他人是自己的真身，不是自己的佣人，更不是自己的敌人。人的野蛮和傲慢源自人对"人"的无知。因此，**"认识人自己"，这是今日人类必须虚心学习的"第一课题"。**

第五，人类成员之黑白黄棕、男女老幼，人性是同一的，人格是平等的，需要是相同的，因而个体的幸福永远是人类的根本；反过来说，人类是由所有个体血肉相连而成的整体，因而类体的安危永远是个体的根本。而这也就是说，人权与类权是人类权力体系中"两极相通"着的两个极地，处于两极之间的政权、主权、领土权、领空权、领海权、财权、军权等等，都是因人权、类权方才产生并为之服务的辅助系统。因此，**任何其它权力都必须服从于、服务于人类的人权和类权，这是21世纪对各类掌权者的"第一命令"。**

这五个"第一"，构成了全球文明的基本理念。

3.　全球文明的来源和框架

人类由三大元素构成：一是物质生活、肉体需要，二是社会生活、情感需要，三是精神生活、信仰需要。因此，文明也有三个组成部分：一是它所体现的世界观及其外化形态，二是它的人类观及其外化形态，三是它的神灵观及其外化形态。

人类在近万年的文明史中，在彼此隔绝的地理条件下，先后创造出了许多优秀的文明模式：古西亚北非文明，印度文明，中华文明，犹太文明，伊斯兰文明，西欧文明，斯拉夫文明，黑非洲文明，日本文明，美国文明，拉丁美洲文明，大洋洲文明，等等。每种文明都表达着各自的人们对于世界、人类、神灵的理解。

如果站在全球时代的角度、站在人类整体的层面，对上述文明进行综合分析，我们可以提取出如下三种最有代表性、最具世界意义和最能引导人类走向美好未来的文明体系：

一是起源于古爱琴文明，定型于古希腊—古罗马文明，完成于近、现代欧洲—北美文明的西方文明。这是一种侧重于人—物关系的文明体系，是一种尊重自然、崇尚财富和注重科学的文明模式。它的主要成果是，建立在世界的决定论与非决定论统一基础上的、展现了"万物共一"理念的世界观。

二是起源于黄河文明，定型于道—儒—佛文明，完成于近、现代东亚—东南亚文明的东方文明。这是一种侧重于人—人关系的文明体系，是一种追求大同、崇尚仁义和注重人学的文明模式。它的主要成果是，建立在人的自然本性与人道本性统一基础上的、体现了"人类共一"理念的人类观。

三是起源于两河文明，定型于古埃及—古希伯来—古巴比伦文明，完成于近现代犹太教—基督教—伊斯兰教文明的中部文明。这是一种侧重于人—神关系的文明体系，是一种敬畏神灵、崇尚灵魂和注重神学的文明模式。它的主要成果是，建立在神灵的超然性与终极性统一基础上的、体现了"众神共一"理念的神灵观。

巧合的是，不少人把西方文明比喻为"蓝色文明"，把东方文明比喻为"黄色文明"，把中部文明比喻为"红色文明"。的确，正是这三大文明模式中的精要部分，构成了全球文明体系的三原色[12]。

---

12 这里有两点需要说明：第一，我们生存在地球，地球是圆的，本不存在西方、东方、中部的划分问题。我们所以从地理上、方位上界定文明，只是沿用了传统上对文明的划分。就是说，我们的目的，只是在深入分析人类各主要文明模式的基础上，提取出组成全球文明的主要成份。第二，我们在对这三个文明体系的界定中，所以要用"侧重于"、"主要成果"这两种限制，是因为每一种文明体系也都包含着其它二者的内容，只是它们处于次要的和从属的位置。

必须指出，西方文明、中部文明、东方文明中的任何一种，都不能视为全球文明精神的基调、主根和主干。把三种文明中的任何一种文明视为主要的、普适的、普世的模式，都会导致文化帝国主义，都会造成人类文明的新灾难。所以这样说，不仅因为上述三种文明都片面强调了"文明三要素"中的一种要素，即用一种要素排斥、贬低和误读另外两种要素，最后反把自己强调的东西推向了负面，还因为人们今天已经十分清楚地看到，西方文明有着把人"物化"的不良元素，中部文明有着把人"神化"的不良元素，东方文明有着把人"异化"的不良元素。

因此，我们不能同意"21世纪将是东方文明的世纪"[13]"21世纪仍是西方文明的世纪"以及"21世纪将是生物学的世纪"、"21世纪将是太空学的世纪"等诸如此类的说法。既然21世纪注定是人类生存的各个方面都将全球化的"全球世纪"，那么，21世纪就只能是全人类共同发展、全面发展、协调发展的世纪，只能是平等发展、和平发展、互为发展的世纪。简言之，21世纪只能是全球发展、文明发展的世纪，只能是让全球都文明起来的世纪。所以，全球文明就是全球文明，它是既来源于整合了上述三大文明理念，又独立于超越了上述三大文明成果的全新形态的文明体系。在这一体系中，西方文明侧重于满足人的自然—肉体—科技的需要，东方文明侧重于满足人的社会—价值—道德的需要，中部文明侧重于满足人的精神—信仰—修为的需要，三者之间既各司其

其它文明，如自成一体的印度文明、成型较晚的日本文明、特色模糊的南美文明、尚在重组中的非洲文明、迅速发育的大洋洲文明，即使不便从地缘和历史上归入上述三大文明之中，仍可以用这三大文明成果所提供的文明标准，对它们的文明特征做出合理的解释，对它们的文明进步提供根本的指导。

13　由于21世纪的个体、群体、民族、国家以及政治、经济、文化、宗教等都将日益全球化，这就使得制订全球交往原则、世界道德规范，确立众生平等、天下一家的生存理念等问题显得格外重要。这种情况使得东方(如季羡林等许多中国学者)、西方(如汤因比等许多西方学者)、中部(如以色列、伊朗的许多学者)即全世界的许多学者，不约而同地看好了五千年来始终以注重社会道德准则、主张世界大同、强调克己奉公著称的"东方文明"。其实，在全球世界形成的初期也许是这样。但从深层、从长远、从整体来看，全球化着的人类自始至终都不能轻视西方文明所强调的物质生活、肉体需要、科学精神，自始至终也离不开中部文明所强调的精神生活、灵魂需要、信仰精神。因此，如果把21世纪判断为"东方文明的世纪"，对于全人类、对于东方人类、特别是对于中华民族来讲，绝不是一件幸事。

任、层面分明，又彼此贯通、互相支撑。

广博而浩瀚的"蓝色海洋"，那是孕育、催生和滋养人类的地方；在蓝色海域的水平面上，突起一片片神奇、鲜活并由绿色覆盖着的"黄色陆地"，那是人类繁衍、生息和成长的乐园；在蓝色海域和黄色地域的上空，有一尊由"红色太阳"代表的神灵，那是照耀、呵护和引领人类的上苍。蓝—黄—红的标志，物—人—神的本质、肉—情—灵的结构，真—善—美的趋向，三种文明要素互相激发、遥相呼应、生机勃勃，这就是全球文明所描绘的21世纪乃至更远未来的人类生存图景。

总之，**西方文明、东方文明、中部文明这三大文明体系的优长部分，即万物共一的世界观、思维观，人类共一的人类观、价值观，众神共一的神灵观、信仰观，相互支撑、彼此促进、三项共构，熔铸成了全球文明的稳固框架。**

二. 分 论

文明，一般说来是指人类在一定时代条件下的生存逻辑。生存逻辑包括思维逻辑、行为逻辑、信仰逻辑三个基本方面。思维逻辑表达着相应的世界观，行为逻辑表达着相应的人类观，信仰逻辑表达着相应的神灵观。

进一步看，任何一种文明都是它的"文明胚"发育的结果。新的文明胚总是产生于相对成熟、逐渐陈旧的文明体系之中。当着一种文明体系不再适合新时代人们的相互交往范围和自我意识水平，新的文明胚就会从中孕育出来，并迅速辐射到政治、经济、文化、价值、生活、交往中去，形成由新文明胚所规定的新文明体系[14]。

应当说，全球文明作为人类新文明体系的文明胚，已经展现在我们

14　作为潜含、孕育着新文明体系的种子、胚芽，文明胚也由三种基本成份统一而成：一是它所提供的世界观念，二是它所坚持的人类观念，三是它所蕴含的神灵观念。这三种成份是构成文明胚的三个相互联系着的"基因段"。一种文明之所以具有它的系统性和鲜明特色，正是这三个文明基因段"三角立体"作用的结果。

的现实生活之中了，这就是西方文明提供的万物共一的世界观念和思维逻辑，东方文明提供的人类共一的人类观念和行为逻辑，中部文明提供的众神共一的神灵观念和信仰逻辑。

1. 万物共一的世界观念和思维逻辑

动物的生存是由食物支配的。人类的生活是由观念支配的。在所有观念中，最基本的观念，是人类对于置身其间的世界的观念。

世界观念的内核是哲学。哲学的思维水平反映着人对世界的认识水平。由于这一点，哲学家们常说，一个民族的素质取决于它的哲学思维能力。西方哲学之父柏拉图，在其《理想国》里甚至认为，真正开明的君主必须是一位"哲学王"。

人类对世界的认识有它自己的运行规则，即人们的认识总是由浅到深、由此及彼。为什么我们存在？因为我们有存在的前提条件、历史条件和现实条件；为什么这些条件存在？这样追寻下去，必然导致寻找最终的决定者。这是思维所以为思维的最基本的逻辑追寻。沿着这种逻辑，便顺理成章地产生了远古时代那些图腾论和还原论、近古时代那些本体论和因果论等"决定论"的世界观念。

然而，由于对世界本原、最终原因的求索历经几千年终无答案，人类便对这种追寻的目标、对自己提问题的方式发生了怀疑，从而在到了近代之后转向了对现实对象、具体事物的认识：一个人、一个民族是怎么样生活和成长的？这个事物、那个事物又是怎么样存在和运动的？正是在对这些具体问题的思考中，形成了关于单体事物、具体对象的内部结构和运动规律的认识。严格意义上的科学便由此而生。由于这种认识排除了该物与它物、该物与它物的它物、该物与人、该物与宇宙本质这类终极存在的内在联系，加之它又适逢人类科技的爆发期从而受到实证思维、分科思维的染指，结果便形成了近代、特别是现代诸如随机论、量子论、概率论、混沌论、虚拟论、自组织论等等"非决定论"的世界观念。

可是，非决定论不仅没有克服决定论的不合理性，反倒排除了它的

合理性；同样，决定论既解释不了非决定论的合理性，又反驳不了它的
不合理性。对这种二律背反的痛苦反思使人们意识到：所以造成这种局
面，是因为决定论、非决定论都轻视了对象之间、对象与原因之间、对
象与可能性之间、对象与未来之间有着一种双向对流的"关系"，不懂
得"关系"不仅是一种"间性存在"、是"场"，而且是一种"力量存
在"、是"能"，不懂得凡是"关系"都是双向的，而且双向的关系性
质是不同的，不懂得同一关系的双向性质的差异正是所有事件的总根
源。由于不懂得这种"关系思维"，所以才形成了远近古代的决定论和
近现代的非决定论这样两种尽管相反、却又同样片面的思维模式。

　　实际上，哲学以外的所有学科都以真实的或假设的"关系者"为对
象，唯独以提供世界观念为己任的哲学是研究"关系"的。寻找本质、
真理、规律，获取智慧、顿悟、高尚，所有这些哲学所追求的东西，无
不存在于"关系"之中。任何人，一旦在研究关系，那便踏入哲学领
地、进行世界观这种性质的思考了。因为关系像只见树动、不见风行
的"风"，具有无影无踪的特征，所以，哲学总是表现为抽象性和思辨
性；因为万事万物的各种力量和特性都必须通过关系表现出来，所以，
关系中隐含了关系者即对象物的全部秘密、操控着关系者的所有能量。

　　因此，从这种关系论的世界观念来看，万事万物无不产生于关系、
存在于关系、消失于关系。而这也就是说，事物在本质上不过是依据纵
横交织的众多关系而存在的一个个关系者、中介体。如果万事万物本质
上属于一个个关系者、中介体，那么，它们就既是被决定的，同时又是
反决定的：一个事物为什么会存在、为什么要这样存在？这是因为它是
先前诸多事物相互作用的产物，是因为它一经产生又要生存在与周围众
多现实事物的相互作用之中，是因为它还要通过与周围事物的相互作用
朝着自己确定的方向发展开去，这使它与生俱来就携有一种自己所以为
自己的决定性——一种由特定的前史、历史、现实、未来所决定的那种
决定性。但是，如果一个事物单单是被决定的，那它只能是一堆既没有
时间、又不能运动的死物，只能是一堆既对它物无用、又无自我价值的
废物。这也就是说，新事物的产生本身不过是旧事物体系中的新因素反
决定于周围现存事物的产物，产生之后又处于反决定于周围既有事物的

关系之中。所以，任何事物与生俱来地还潜含着一种对于作为母体的决定者以及周围各种决定者的反决定性，必然要以反决定者的姿态与所有决定者相互作用，这种作用对于决定者和反决定者来说，无疑是一种反决定性质的作用。

问题在于，事物的这种决定性是以反决定性为内在活力的，其反决定性也是以被决定为内在前提的，二者是一体化着的，是"决定－反决定"的，是同一个关系的双重属性。决定者只有内含了反决定因子、存在于众多反决定因素之中，才配称决定者；反决定只有严格限定在决定者的规定之内、不可超出决定性一丝一毫，才配称反决定。这也就是说，万事万物与生俱来就具有一种规定自己存在、使自己因此而成为自己的、现实而又具体的决定－反决定本性。正是这种决定反决定本性，使得事物之间、一事物诸要素之间，在内在形式上必然表现为对立统一规律、阴阳生克规律所描述的情形，在发展过程上必然表现为质量互变规律、否定之否定规律所描述的情形，在外在形态上必然表现为相互作用规律、作用反作用规律所描述的情形。因此，离开决定反决定的所谓"决定"一定是毫无生命活力的无水之河，离开决定反决定的所谓"反决定"又一定是毫无内在规则的无河之水；同样，离开决定反决定的辩证法一定是随心所欲的变戏法，离开决定反决定的矛盾论又一定是失去内在规定的诡辩论；甚至，物质、运动、场、时空等这些最基本的存在，如果不用决定反决定思维去理解，也无法得出哪怕接近客观的认识。

显而易见，这种名为"决定－反决定论"的新哲学思维、新世界观念，既揭示了事物的本性、关系的性质、运动的动因和动力、过程的规则和趋向，又体现了造物主赋予万事万物的那种宇宙本性、那种宇宙精神。我们这个大千世界的许多重大问题清楚了：(1)由于决定性，宇宙及万物才表现出了必然性、确定性、统一性、秩序性、整体性、方向性；(2)由于同时又具有反决定性，宇宙及万物又展现出了运动性、活跃性、新奇性、可能性、发散性、多向性；(3)正是在决定与反决定相互作用的交错点、汇集点、作用点上，创生了宇宙，设定了宇宙及万物的动因、动力、界限、戒线、规律和方向，形成了宇宙及万物的结构性和统一性以及运动性和趋向性，产生了令人类千百年来困惑不解的"空间"和"时间"。比如，爱因斯坦的相对论所以是一个极其伟大的发现，惟在于狭义相对论如实地反映了在确定的参照系中物体的质量、能量、速度、时间、空间之间的决定反决定关系；其广义相对论则如实地反映了任何参照系下它们的决定反决定关系[15]。

决定反决定的意义是显然的。第一，它告别了千百年来总是把关系者之间仅仅视为相互关联、相互作用等等这类直观性和表面化的思维方式，确立了关系者之间严格遵循决定反决定这一互为确证、彼此支撑的，展现了内在规定和深层秩序的思维方式。所谓认识和把握事物，也就寻找和确定它的各种决定者、反决定者，把握它们之间的决定反决定关系。比如父与子，按照决定反决定规则，它们无不在受物种特性、时代条件、社会状况、家庭结构等因素决定，并且无时无刻不在反决定于这些决定因素的决定反决定作用中，才能产生、才能沟通、才能发

---

15 爱因斯坦相对论既不是决定论理论，也不是非决定论理论，而是迄今为止与决定反决定论最为接近的一种理论。

相对论第一次从物理学角度、以数学的方式证明，决定性、决定作用因反决定性、反决定作用而具有相对性，反决定性、反决定作用因决定性、决定作用也具有相对性。所以，相对性是决定反决定性的物理形式和外在形态，决定反决定论则是相对论的理论根据和内在本质。人们可以说：因为物体之间具有决定反决定性，所以表现出了狭义的和广义的相对性；却不能反过来说：因为对象间具有相对性，所以才表现出了决定反决定性。这种逻辑上的不同层级和理论上的不可逆性说明，相对论只回答了对象间"是不是相对的"问题，而决定反决定论则回答了相对论的根源：(1)"谁与谁相对？"(在物理上、形式上它表现为相对论所说的物体的质量、能量、速度、时空之间的相对性；在物性上、根源上则表现为决定者对被决定者的决定性和决定作用是相对的，被决定者对决定者的反决定性和反决定作用是相对的)；(2)"怎么样相对？"(决定者中包含着自己的反决定者，反决定者的反决定性、反决定作用只能在决定者限定的范围之内)；(3)"为什么相对？"(因为决定者必须以自己的反决定者为存在前提、决定作用内含了反决定作用这个前提，所以决定者对被决定者的决定性和决定作用是相对的；因为被决定者的反决定作用不能一味地反击和否定决定者，即必须在决定者限定的范围之内进行，所以，反决定者的反决定性和反决定作用也只能是相对的)。

更为重要的是，相对论为人们提供的是一个相对性的物理世界，而决定反决定论则通过爱因斯坦的相对论、牛顿的绝对论、玻尔的量子论、哥德尔不完全定律、霍金的黑洞论、哥德巴赫的猜想、以及黑格尔的绝对理念和老子的道论的整合，为人们提供了一种动态的、确定的决定—反决定的或曰"超决定"、"自决定"的世界观念，特别是为人们揭示了宇宙生成之源、宇宙秩序之本、宇宙演进之魂和宇宙结局之果。

展。反决定者不断通过众多决定者确立自己的本性和规则，决定者不断从反决定者那里汲取新奇和可能，双双良性互证，这是多么完美的宇宙秩序！因此，决定反决定作为一项揭示了宇宙本性的结构原则，它为人们提供的是一种秩序的人生、秩序的社会、秩序的宇宙。

第二，它告别了千百年来总是把关系者之间视为对立统一、否定之否定等等这类斗争性和革命化的思维方式，确立了关系者之间严格遵循决定反决定这一互为关系、互补规则的，展现了和谐性和共生化的思维方式。这也就是说，所谓认识和把握事物，也就是寻找深藏在决定者与反决定者之间的和谐通道和共生机制。还比如父与子，按照决定反决定规律，它们之间无论如何也不是对立的统一关系、否定之否定的关系，相反，它们只能是互证、互为、互相补宜的互补关系，只能是相爱、相生、相依为命的肯定之肯定的关系。反决定者不断从众多决定者那里得到呵护和营养，决定者不断从反决定者那里得到尊重和满足，双双良性互补，这是多么和谐的宇宙图景！因此，决定反决定作为一条揭示了宇宙演进的作用规律，它为人们提供的是一个和谐的人生、和谐的社会、和谐的宇宙。

第三，它告别了千百年来总是把关系者之间视为相互制约、彼此折磨、互为障碍等等这类消极性和颓废化的思维方式，确立了关系者之间严格遵循决定反决定这一互相促进、互为创造的，展现了积极性和创造性的思维方式。仍比如父与子，按照决定反决定原理，人们总是发现他们彼此都在积极的、创造性的道路上携手并肩，相反，习以为常的众多相互折磨、彼此伤害的事实，完全是由上述那种陈旧的思维方式造成的。反决定者不断从众多决定者那里获得支持和动力，决定者不断从反决定者那里获得新素和活力，双双良性互动，这是多么生动的宇宙前景！因此，决定反决定作为一种揭示了宇宙进步的发展原理，它为人们提供的是一种积极的人生、积极的社会、积极的宇宙。

由此可见，决定反决定性既是宇宙得以生成的"宇宙因"，也是宇宙得以确立的"宇宙魂"，还是宇宙因此而朝向自己确定结局的"宇宙果"。是的，纵观宇宙万有，可以大致分为物能、场能、灵能三大类。照此讲，宇宙及万事万物的真正的和共同的本质是"能量"即"能"。

而能量所以为能量，恰恰由于能量本身就是具有决定反决定性质的"序动态"。

总之，由于万物无不具有决定反决定的本性，无不处在网络有序的决定反决定关系之中，所以，宇宙必然是一个有机的体系，万事万物之间也必然是一种共一的关系。就是说，所谓万物共一的"一"，就是深藏在万事万物内里、规定着它们的存在、联系和发展的那种决定反决定本性。也正是因为万事万物无不秉有决定反决定本性，无不处在纵横交织、环环相扣的决定反决定作用之中，所以它们只能是不同而又相关、独立而又相生的。显而易见，这种决定反决定论的世界观念、思维逻辑，既继承了历史上各种决定论的合理性，又继承了各种非决定论的合理性，既否定了传统世界观念中那种单极的思维逻辑、对立的思维模式、物质化的思维框架、本体论的思维习惯，又高扬了在关系中实现觉悟、在关系中寻找真理、在关系中发掘未来的世界观天性。因此，这种"决定－反决定论"，就是我们从西方文明、特别是从西方的"决定论"和"非决定论"的哲学－科学成果中，提炼出来的全新的世界观念和思维逻辑。

万物共一，就其普泛性而言，就是物物共一；就其深刻性而言，就是物性共一。

我们认为，这种揭示了万物共一的"决定－反决定论"的物性学说、事物理念，立足关系的认识原则，就是西方文明为全球文明提供的世界观念和思维逻辑。

2.　人类共一的人类观念和行为逻辑

人类对自己的理解是怎样的，生存理念就是怎样的。人的自我意识是其人生活动、价值取向、社会行为的根源。"认识你自己"，这句产生于两千多年前的古训，似乎到今天才具有了现实的意义。

那么，"人类"究竟是什么呢？认识人的真正难点，在于用什么样的方式认识人、以什么为参照系解释人。千百年来，人们总是用人与动物、人与神灵相比较的方式界定人，总是以人的派生物——如家庭、社会、国家、劳动、工具、文化、宗教——为参照系解释人。于是，在人类自我认识史上，便顺理成章地产生了如下的结论：(1)人是有理智的、没有羽毛的、两条腿走路的、有情感的"动物"，(2)人是文化性的、政治性的、社会性的、主体性的大自然的主人即"圣物"，(3)人是一半天使一半野兽的"怪物"。

其实，我们既不能升到天国去理解神灵，也无法屈居洞穴来理解动物。与不理解的东西相比较来界定人，这本身就是一大逻辑错误。同样，我们也不能以人类活动的产物即派生物为参照系来界定人，人类活动的派生物是一定历史阶段中人类自我意识的外化形态，用派生物界定原生物，也不合乎逻辑。错误逻辑必然导致错误推论。所以，把人界定为动物、圣物、怪物，都是错误的。

这也就是说，我们必须运用关系论的世界观念和决定反决定论的思维方式才能解释人，即在兽、人、神的决定反决定关系中认识人；必须以创造了人类并赋于其人性的宇宙本性为参照系才能认清人，也就是从人类对自身的宇宙本性的体悟中才能认清自己。

倘若如此，我们可以发现一个极其简单却又最为深刻的事实：人类的本性乃是一种"自然－人道性"。

人从出于自然、生活于自然、消失于自然，所以人有着先天的自然本性。这里的道理非常简单，人诞生在自然之中、动物之后，必然具有自然的本性、带有动物的胎记。人的这种自然本性、动物形态是人所为人的前提、基础和载体。但是，人一经脱离动物界，成为在生命级上高于动物兽性的生命种群，便会居高临下地极力排斥自身的兽性。为了挣脱兽性，人在生活中按照自己的人性向往和对造物主的体悟，发现并确立了一种高于自己的存在——神灵。通过信仰神灵升入"人道"，从此沿着"人道——人的道路"前进，这是人类摆脱自身兽性的一次伟大而成功的创举。

问题在于，人的自然本性与人道本性是一体化着的、是"自然－人道"性质的。只有被人道化了的自然本性，才是人的本性，否则就是兽性；也只有被自然化了的人道本性，才是人的本性，否则就是神性。这就是说，被神性化了的兽性或被兽性化了的神性，正是人类的人性；这种兽－人－神三项缘构的特殊的地球生命物种就是人类。如果从哲学、文化学、人类学、人性学上作学理上的表述，我们人类乃是一种"具有自然－人道性质的地球生物"。自然－人道性是宇宙本性的人性形式，这同宇宙本性在石头那里表现为简单存在性、在植物那里表现为一般生长性、在动物那里表现为肉体活动性是一个道理。

在前面"全球文明的含义"中，我们把人类的属性解释为人性与类性的整合、把人类的存在解释为个体与类体的统一、把人类的进化解释为生性与生境的互塑。所以如此，也是由于我们把人类的本性界定为自然－人道性的原故。就是说，自然－人道性，这是人类的人性－类性属性、个体－类体生存、生性－生境互动的共同根源。

上述分析说明什么呢？它说明：

我们是人，不是动物！绝不能把人类界定为弱肉强食、茹毛饮血的动物！

我们是人，不是圣物！也不能把人类界定为唯我独尊、主宰众生的圣物！

我们是人，不是怪物！更不能把人类界定为忽而动物、忽而圣物的怪物！

我们是人，人只是人！只是自然被人道化、人道被自然化着的地球生物！

我们还可以从人类的生命特征上作进一步地分析。

人类所以与动物和神灵有着本质的不同，是因为动物和神灵只经历一次生成，而人类则要经历两次生成。一棵树、一只猫，从生到死没有本质的变化；任何一种宗教所信奉的神灵，都是永生、永在的，也不能变化。与之不同，人则要经历"自发"和"自觉"两次生成。

以我们人类的个体成长为例——

每个正常人都要经历两次生成，并且每个生成期又分为两个成长阶段。

经历第一次生成的第一个阶段，人从自然、从父母那里获得了人的自然生命体，这是人之谓人的载体、前提和基础，这个阶段包括配子期、胎儿期、婴儿期；第二个成长阶段是从家庭、社会、时代、劳动、交往、教育中获得人之为人的特征、特性和特质，这个阶段包括童年时代、少年时代、青年时代。经过这次生成，人便完成了从动物人到正常人的人生使命。

更为重要的是第二次生成。在第二次生成的第一阶段，人要通过对自己作为人的"人性"和作为人类整体一份子的"类性"及其关系的理解和把握，通过对人－人关系、天－人关系、身－心关系的洞察和定位，自觉使自己成为人，成为能用正确的人性意识支配自己生命活动的人，成为既实现了自我又贡献于社会的人，这个阶段包括中年时代和壮年时代。第二次生成的第二个阶段是人对晚年和死亡成熟的认识和把握，即把晚年视为最成熟的、肩负着教育人类的、更应当无愧于人的人生阶段，把死亡视为宇宙内、人世间、人生中最深沉最伟大的一种转化、一种进化、一种使命、一种贡献、一种新生、一种永生[16]。

因此，如果说人类个体的第一次生成要完成人≠动物的人生使命，那么，第二次生成则要实现人＝"人"的人生飞跃。

我们人类的类体生成也是这样——

自20世纪末叶人类进入全球世界和信息时代算起，在此之前的漫长历史都属于第一次生成期，即自发的生成期。在这一次生成中，长达四百多万年的整个原始人的历史，属于第一次生成的第一个阶段；近五千年的文明史特别是公元元年前后两千年左右的历史，构成了第二个阶段。经历这次生成，人类学会了直立行走、用火、制造工具、语言、结社、法律、文明、良知，等等。所以，这次生成是"人类"作为人科、人种、人属即"人"的生成。

从20世纪末开始，现在我们看得越来越清楚，人类正在进入第二个生成期。这次生成将是人类作为宇宙间唯一一种"类体生物"的生成，也就是"人类"之"类"的生成。

经历第二次生成的第一个阶段，人类将摆脱单体性、群体性甚至血缘性、氏族性、种族性的支配和制约，使人类真正自觉认识到自己是一种"类体生物"，从而使每个人都能按照"类本性"的要求思想、生活、劳动和交往。所以，这个阶段的主要内容，如前所述，是学会人人平等、世界和平、天下一家，学会作世界公民、地球之子，学会全球文

---

16 人类历史上产生的那些圣人、智者、圣雄、觉者，所以表现出伟大的、超常的、高尚的人格，就是因为他们在经历了从动物人到正常人的人生磨砺即第一次生成之后，又完成了从自发人到自觉人的升华即第二次生成。

明，学会用文明的方式推进文明。应当说，这是人类进化史上继往开来的大事件，也是宇宙演化史上激动人心的大飞跃。显然，第二次生成的第一个阶段，是"人类自觉成为类"的阶段。

此后，人类还要按照宇宙精神赋于人类的另一项使命，完成第二次生成的第二个阶段——"人类自觉否定类"的阶段。在这个阶段，人类将自觉遵循自然－人道主义的进化方向，用自己的智慧和双手，以心甘情愿否定自己的伟大胸襟缔造出超人类，从而使宇宙演化、地球文明进入比"人类生命级"更为高级的阶段——超人类阶段。心甘情愿的否定自己，这是宇宙赋于人类的最高使命，这是人类最可引以为豪的事情，同时也是宇宙演进的最高境界。应当说，生命科学特别是人类基因测序工程、转基因技术、干细胞技术、端粒技术和克隆技术的高速发展，宇宙科学特别是理论物理学、高能物理学、UFO研究和太空技术的突飞猛进，尤其是人对宇宙生成原因、构成机制、演进秩序、最终结局及其所蕴含的宇宙精神越来越深刻的认知，对自己肩负的人类自我进化责任、地球文明进化责任和推进宇宙演进责任的觉悟，已经预示出了这一辉煌的生成阶段。

因此，如果说人类的第一次生成是要实现人类≠人种的伟大进程，那么，第二次生成则要完成人类="人类"的庄严使命。

总之，我们是人，人类只有一群，所以必须团结；人性只有一种，所以必须平等；地球只有一个，所以必须保护；人生只有一次，所以必须认真；生命只有一瞬，所以必须珍惜。这种种唯一性，要求今天的人类必须确立人类共一的人类观念和行为原则[17]。而在这种种的唯一中，最根本的是人性共一。所以，人类共一的"一"，就是人所为人的自然－人道性。由于人人无不具有同一种自然－人道本性，因而人类真正

17　如此说来，历史上曾存的、现时代正存的几乎所有的人类观念、人性意识，都是异化的、错位的。这种异化和错位，使得今天的人类已经成了地球上一个最愚蠢、最野蛮的生命种群。比如，人类的核力量，已经能将60亿的人类毁灭60次，这既是铁一般的事实，又违反着"人生不是为了死亡"、"死亡无法重复"这些最基本的逻辑；再如，国家与国家之间的真正关系竟然成了杀人的军事能力的对比关系；又如，金钱、色情、破坏竟然成了支撑人类生存的三脚架、推动人类进步的主动力；还如，谁是富翁谁就当然的既可以呼唤政治家、军事家，又可以雇佣哲学家、神学家的主子，如此等等。

的出路只能是平等、互补，只能是团结、共生，只能是"己所不欲，勿施于人"、"己所欲者，更予于人"。因此，这种"自然－人道论"，就是我们从东方文明、特别是从"道法自然"、"人者，仁也"、"众生平等"的道学－儒学－佛学成果中，提炼出来的全新的人类观念和行为逻辑。

人类共一，就其普泛性而言，就是人人共一；就其深刻性而言，就是人性共一。

我们认为，这种揭示了人类共一的"自然－人道论"的人性学说、社会理念，立足天下一家的价值原则，就是东方文明为全球文明提供的人类观念和行为逻辑。

3.　　众神共一的神灵观念和信仰逻辑

肉身是人类的载体，社会是人类的介体，精神是人类的本体[18]。人

---

18 能不能认清和把握"肉体是人类的载体，社会是人类的介体，精神是人类的本体"，是人类成熟与否的重要的——毋宁说是唯一的标志。围绕着人类的"肉体"，形成了一个庞大的自然科学家群体；围绕着人类的"社会"，形成了一个庞大的政治家、社会科学家群体；围绕着人类的"精神"，形成了一个庞大的精神－心理学家、神学－宗教学家群体。可是，我们看到，这些学问家和实践家们，要么割裂了肉体、社会、精神的内在联系，要么错解了甚至颠倒了载体、介体、本体的位置，从而把人类的思维引向一种又一种误区和错误，把人类的生活引向一个又一个苦难和灾难。

在我们看来，人类不同于动物、高级于动物的根本原因，不仅是由于人类具有构建复杂而精密的社会并以此为"介体"的能力，更是因为人类倒转了动物的意识与肉体的主次关系，选择了以精神为本体的生物进化道路。由此可见，造物主创造人类的主要目的并不是让人类比动物更野蛮的破坏自然、自相残杀，而是(1)通过这种"以精神为本体"的地球智力生物来提升宇宙演进的层级，即把宇宙的物理性自发性演化升级为生物性自觉性演化；(2)以此展现出深藏在宇宙深处的那种"以物能为载体、以场能为介体、以灵能为本体"的宇宙奥秘。

是的，宇宙从产生到今日直到永远，它都是以自己的物能为载体、场能为介体、灵能为本体的。如果宇宙演化不以自己的精神这一灵能为主导、为本体，宇宙及万物就不可能展现出精美的结构性、确定的过程性和明确的目的性。而人类这里的"肉体－社会－精神"的构件及其"载体－介体－本体"的构架，不过是宇宙那种"物能－场能－灵能"构件和"以物能为载体、以场能为介体、以灵能为本体"这种构架的人类化。对于这一点，可参阅本节下文和结论中的注释。

类精神的核心是信仰。人们信仰什么，他们的世界观念、人类观念就是怎样的。世界观念是神灵观念的物理—道理形式，人类观念是神灵观念的心理—伦理形式。正因为如此，人们才有这种相同而深刻的感受：人生最大的悲哀根源于没有信仰，人间最大的悲剧来自于错误信仰，人类最大的罪过莫过于利用信仰[19]。

信仰，无论是祖先崇拜、英雄崇拜、先知崇拜等人格化信仰，还是图腾崇拜、民族崇拜、理想崇拜等非人格化信仰，被信仰者对于信仰者即人来说，都是超然性、终极性、至上性、唯一性存在，都是主宰信众、使人敬畏、给人希望的神圣存在，即都属于创造了信众从而"高于信众生存级"因而能够福佑信众的神灵性质的存在。

人的神灵观念直接表现为人的精神境界。精神境界的"境"是指精神的情境、意境，精神境界的"界"是指精神的界域、界位。所以，精神境界是人的自我认识成熟程度的根据，是人的人性纯洁程度的尺度，是人对世界理解程度的标志，是人的胸襟敞阔程度的根源[20]。

从逻辑上讲，人的精神境界应当是人的所思、所言、所欲、所为都无愧于"人"的境界。所谓无愧于人的境界，就是人对自己的理解无愧于人，人在宇宙间的自我定位无愧于人，个人与个人、人群与人群、国家与国家之间的各种交往无愧于人，人与生境——自然生境、社会生境、心理生境的相互作用无愧于人，在处理灵与肉、欲与义、情与理的

---

19 应当说，利益的纷争是表层的纷争，文化的差异是中层的差异，信仰的冲突才是根本的冲突。甚至可以这样说，宗教信仰不仅能够改变信众的政治、经济和文化，而且可以改变信众的人口密度、人性纯度和人种特征。

20 如此说来，各种各样的很低劣的精神境界，至今还充斥于今天的人世间。在某些西方国家，人的自由变成了自由地胡作非为、胡作非为的自由，人的平等变成了平等地走向两极分化、走入人格分裂。在某些东方国家，人的道德变成了毫无人格可言的血缘性忠孝和等级性依附，人的情感几乎整个地陷入了血统情结、乡土情结、民粹情结。在某些宗教里，贴的是普渡众生、慈悲天下的标签，干的却是仇视异教、铲除异己的勾当。在某些百姓中，精神界域就是狭小的三丈住宅，精神意境就是尽可能再厚一些的纸币。哲学家们的精神境界看起来非常高尚，其实，许多哲学家只是在宣泄小小自我的幽幽之情，或者是为总统总理的政治主张寻找哲学上的证明。政治家们的精神境界似乎很是堂皇，其实，不少政治家真正关注的，是屁股下面那把木质的或镶了珠宝的木质的座椅、特别是座次。

关系时无愧于人。

那么，怎么样做才能无愧于人呢？"怎么做"的实质是"为什么这么做"，"为什么这么做"的实质是"人是什么"，而"人是什么"的实质又是"人为什么是这样"。所以，真正的问题是：人与创造了自己的造物主、人与赋于了自己人性的宇宙本性，从而与生存其间的这个世界是什么关系。

我们人类，是宇宙在按照自己精神的演进过程中，在经历了无机阶段、有机阶段、肉体阶段之后，又到达了我们"人类"这样一个全新的阶段——肉体-智力生命阶段，亦即自然-人道性阶段。我们的肉体是宇宙按照自己的精神演化出来的一种产物，我们的智力也是宇宙按照自己的精神演化出来的一种产物，我们的肉体和智力具有决定反决定性质的自然-人道关系，是宇宙按照自己的精神演化出的又一种产物。

这就提出了"什么是宇宙精神"的问题。

宇宙在自己的演进过程中，展示出一种最为强大的力量、最为博大的情怀、最为伟大的意志。这种力量、情怀、意志，可以用哲学家的逻辑推理出来，用科学家的仪器测量出来，用神学家的灵觉感悟出来，用我们普通人的经验体味出来。科学家们把这种力量、情怀、意志定义为公理、原理、定理、规律，神学家们把它奉之为上帝、真主、佛、道，哲学家们把它称之为存在的存在、思维的思维、道德的道德、自由的自由，百姓们把它解释为天然、天性、天理、天道。

从今天的人类认识水平看，宇宙演进所展示出来的这种宇宙力量、宇宙情怀、宇宙意志，乃是一种宇宙的终极精神实在，一种"宇宙精神"。所谓"宇宙力量"，就是使宇宙得以存在和演进的内驱力、结构力和牵引力；所谓"宇宙情怀"，就是宇宙把最大事物与最小事物、最远事物与最近事物、最高事物与最低事物统一起来，把宇宙的本与末、一与多、形而上与形而下统一起来的情怀；所谓"宇宙意志"，就是宇宙注定被创生出来的必然性，就是宇宙规定自己存在的确定性，就是使事物的潜能和可能在与它物相互作用中被激活、被唤醒、被生发的新奇性，就是使事物通过与外物的相互作用使自己不断超越自己的超越性。

这种宇宙力量、宇宙情怀、宇宙意志的统一就是宇宙精神[21]。而这种宇宙精神，细细想来，正是千百年来人类所敬畏的"神"或"神灵"，正是基督教徒所说的"上帝"、伊斯兰教徒所说的"真主"、佛教徒所说的"佛"。

宇宙精神既是宇宙演进的启动器、发动机和设计图，还是它的方向盘、路线图和目的地。宇宙在宇宙精神这种多重力量的作用下，在演进到距今40多亿年的时候，产生了我们这个地球。在距今30多亿年的时候，滋育出了地球生命。在距今500多万年的时候，创生了人类这一迄今所知唯一一种肉体—智力生命群体。在距今一万年的时候，创造出了作为人类定型标志的文明。到了今天，它又为人类确立了标志人类成熟的进化方向——全球文明的进化方向。

爱因斯坦说，我不相信干预人类正当事务的上帝，我信仰斯宾诺莎的上帝。他在晚年还说，在宇宙的深处，有一种神秘而又神圣的力量在操纵着这个宇宙，我不能认清它，无法解释它，但我承认它、敬畏它。著名的英国历史学家汤因比，更加明确地把宇宙精神表述为"人类在其中得以自我感知的宇宙内部及其背后的那个终极精神实在"，他还非常

---

21 宇宙是有精神的。我们人类的精神根本说来就是宇宙精神的一种特化形态——地球人类精神形态。精神，这是一种意识性、认知性、自知性、自觉性、自为性的力量或"能"。宇宙从一开始就必须有一种支配自己的精神，否则，它就不能作为一种瓜熟蒂落的实在被创造出来，不能作为一个网络有序的整体存在下来，也不能作为一种有条不紊的过程发展开去，更不能不偏不倚地走向自己的结局；宇宙精神还必须是宇宙中唯一的、终极的、至高无上的实在，否则，它就不能创造万有、主宰一切，不配称上帝、真主。

是的，比如上帝、真主，它之所以被它的信徒们公认为是造物主、主宰者，就是因为它是一种宇宙的意识、宇宙的精神。所以，从精神看宇宙，宇宙是受自己精神规定和支配的能量体系；从宇宙看精神，精神乃是指挥着宇宙机体正常运行的一种意识，是宇宙最深刻的本质，也是宇宙最根本的部分。离开精神的宇宙，只是一片死寂；离开宇宙的精神，只是人对自己粗陋智力错误的类比、延伸和推论。所以，宇宙精神，一言以蔽之，就是具有精神的宇宙与支配宇宙的精神的统一，所以在本文中简称为"宇宙—精神"。

退一步说，正如只有物理规律可以解释物理变化、只有化学规律可以解释化学变化一样，只有精神规律才能解释精神现象。这样一来，要想解释我们人类的精神，就必须依照宇宙的精神才有可能。因为，人类精神说到底也是宇宙演进到一定阶段的产物，说到底也只能是宇宙精神的"人类形态"。

深刻地把索罗亚斯德、毕达哥拉斯、"以赛亚"第二、释迦牟尼、孔子等先知界定为"他们每一个个人都与人类在其中得以自我感知的宇宙内部及其背后的那个终极精神实在，建立了直接的私人关系。"[22] 爱因斯坦理解的"上帝"，汤因比表述的那种"终极精神实在"，就是这里所说的宇宙精神。

如果具体一些，我们可以对宇宙精神作这样的分述——

(1)宇宙精神是使宇宙在经历了纯自然性的诸如物理阶段、微生物阶段、植物阶段、动物阶段之后，又进一步在人类这里展现出了自然－人道本性之自然－人道主义精神，或"超自然精神"。

(2)宇宙精神是启悟人类通过自己的智慧和双手，以心甘情愿否定自己的胸襟使宇宙到达超人类阶段的精神，或"超人类精神"。

(3)宇宙精神是创生出人类智力并给了智力以自创造能力，从而使智力通过自创造活动不断由一种智力水平到达更高水平之智力所以为智力的精神，或"超智力精神"。

(4)宇宙精神是使宇宙在本质上表现为能量，使能量分级为物能、场能、灵能，并使这三类能量既彼此成立又相互催化之能量所以为能量的精神，或"超能量精神"。

(5)宇宙精神是使万物呈现为过程，使彼此不同或前后不同过程的相互作用过程又呈现出进化特征之进化过程的进化的精神，或"超进化精神"。

(6)宇宙精神是使宇宙及万物通过决定性表现出整体、统一和秩序，通过反决定性展现出发展、新奇和超越的决定反决定精神，或"超决定精神"。

(7)宇宙精神是使事物发展遵循着确定的规律，使不同规律之间的相互作用又遵循着确定规律之规律所以为规律的精神，或"超规律精神"。

(8)宇宙精神是使宇宙在人类面前表现为无数神秘现象组成的体系，使神秘经过人类的认知和验证成为科学知识，从而使宇宙精神通过神

22　《人类与大地母亲》〔英〕阿诺德•汤因比著，中译本，ISBN-7-208-03809-0，第157页。

学与科学的日趋接近呈现其"神圣实在"之科学所以为科学的精神，或"超科学精神"。

综上，宇宙精神是创生了宇宙、分化出万有、引领着所有的精神，是宇宙间唯一的、至高的、神圣的、精神的实在，是人类千百年来所信奉的上帝、真主、佛等众多不同信主本质特性的整合。

回顾人类宗教史，犹太教通过对民族历史中神迹的反思领悟到了上帝，伊斯兰教通过对偶像崇拜教训的总结感悟到了真主，佛教通过对生命本质的剖析感觉到了佛，道教通过对自然法则的追寻理解到了道，儒教通过对人生真谛的求索寻找到了仁，如此等等。它们的感受是不相同的，更是不相容的。然而，我们每一个直面全球时代的人，每一个没有偏见成见的人，每一个希冀世界和平的人，都能共同地感受到宇宙精神展现出来的全面性、深刻性和共一性，都会对宇宙精神引领人类沿着氏族——民族——国家——国家联盟的道路，最后实现天下一家、世界大同、万教归宗的坚定意志，有着相同的认识。

从更深的层面看，宗教乃是人类生存体系中最为复杂的文明现象：第一，每个宗教都是人类、特别是创教者个人在特定时代对神灵或宇宙本性的理解，因而宗教信仰难免要受到民族进程、人类进化阶段等历史条件的限制，受到创教者、继承者等个人能力的局限；第二，宗教所以为宗教，是因为它那强劲的根须是深扎在信主的至上性、唯一性和终极性之中的，这就使一些真知和启示一旦凝聚为教义，便获得了恒久的特点；第三，宗教信仰从来都是统一信众思维、控制信众灵魂的特殊力量，这一特点又使宗教信仰对于人类来说，有着根本上的支配性。这样一来，宗教教义中本来正常的历史局限，宗教经典中难以避免的些微不足，宗教教主因诚信信主而自然形成的思维侧重不同、前后表述不一、乃至性格特点上的细小疵疵，都会随着社会进步、时代变迁和信众扩大而被放大、扭曲、变质，久而久之便由正而偏、由偏而错、由错而恶，最后沦为邪教，甚至酿成巨大的"宗教悲剧"、"信仰灾难"[23]。与之

---

23 举例来说，有的宗教至今还把信条植根在民族古老的历史恩怨之中、特别是扎根在人性的原始本能之中，强化着"非我族类其心必异"、"敌人的敌人正是朋友"、"狭路相逢勇者胜"等等人的劣根性，把社会推入阵发性的动荡之中，而社会越

不同，我们每一个有正常思维能力的人，每一个有现代文明常识的人，每一个良知尚存的人，都会对宇宙精神那种近500万年来始终都在引领人类朝向真、善、美、优、乐，一直都在帮助人类挣脱假、恶、丑、劣、苦的强大力量、博大情怀、伟大意志，有着相同的体验。

我们可以将这种认识再推进一步。把宇宙精神解释为超自然、超人类、超智力、超能量、超进化、超决定、超规律、超科学的终极精神实在，其实也就是说：(1)宇宙精神揭示了诸如自然、人类、智力、能量等等的共同根源，所以它是宇宙中最初始、最终极的部分；(2)宇宙精神还体现了它们的共同本质，所以它是宇宙中最根本、最神圣的部分；(3)如果宇宙精神既是它们的共同根源，又是它们的共同本质，那么，它就是融通宇宙－人类－神灵、沟通科学－人学－神学、打通历史－现实－未来、贯通真实－善良－美好的唯一力量。巧合的是，这里所说的神圣性、终极性、全能性，正是上帝、真主、佛的共同特征。如果是这样，那么，我们用这种宇宙精神就可以很容易地解释各大宗教那千姿百态的信仰特点和历史特征，很容易地发现它们背后的相同追求和共同本质，很容易地把握它们之间的互补性与和合性。宗教已经有了长达十万年的历史，严格意义上的宗教也已积累了近五千年的经验，特别是近二千年来，随着社会的前进、交往的拓展，人类更有数不胜数的宗教对立、宗教战争的惨痛教训。面对今天的全球世界，面对今天的文明水平，人类有责任把自己对神灵的解释、对宗教信仰的理解、对不同宗教之间关系的处理方式提升一步。

这也就是说，生活在21世纪的人类，特别是世界各大宗教中那些虔诚的宗教徒，不是抛弃而要更加刻苦地同时研读和理解《圣经》、《古兰经》、《金刚经》等等，不是怀疑而要更加清醒地分辨和把握众先知

是动荡，它就越发亢奋，越具有生命力和破坏性；又如，有的宗教至今仍在教化信众悲观愤世，消极厌世，寻求避世，坐等来世；还如，有的宗教无视科学常识、人类进步，仍在诱导信众沉迷巫术、方术、编织幻觉、神迹，追逐玄秘、怪力。更有甚者，有的宗教信仰在今天只剩下了清规戒律、朝拜祈祷、焚香叩头、科仪服饰等宗教外壳，在这样的宗教里，不少教徒已经堕落成了全靠吸吮社会肌体鲜血为生的寄生虫，退化成了煽动恐怖、注射仇恨、策动暴力、制造动乱的教唆犯，其宗教场所也变成了滋生贫困、愚昧、专制、血腥、淫乱、战争的温床。

的背景、语境和本意，不是改变而是更加坚定地信奉和敬畏上帝、真主、佛等等，不是反对而是更加自觉地成为全球时代的新型的有神论者。因为，正是这些伟大而不朽的先知和他们的经典，从不同层面，用不同表述，揭示了宇宙、地球、人类、生命、精神、神灵的真相，并因此获得了在今天的全球时代教化全人类的资格；因为，正是"上帝"教、"真主"教、"佛"教等几大世界性宗教，在彼此不同的时空里，以各自的方式，从特定的角度，最早、最明确、也最准确地确立了以宇宙精神为宗教基础和信仰内涵的信主的至上地位，并因此至今征服着亿万信众。

总之，众神共一的"一"就是宇宙精神。所谓众神共一，就是人类所信仰的古往今来、千差万别的神灵，都是同一个人类的不同人群对同一种宇宙精神的不同理解和不同称谓。进一步讲，只要能够完整的体现宇宙精神，能够沟通和统一全人类的精神信仰，众神共一"共"在上帝、"共"在真主、"共"在佛，只是代名词的选择问题，又有什么关系！当然，如果因此而去争抢这个位置，那就正好背离了宇宙精神，误解了本教的基本教义，曲解了本教创教人的本意，也就有罪于全体人类、有悖于全球时代了。因此，宇宙精神论是一种面向全人类的科学－人学－神学结论，而不是集中一群人去对付另一群人的宗教理论；宇宙精神信仰是一种精神信仰和信仰思维，而不是任何意义的宗教信仰和新派宗教。显然，只有在这种"宇宙精神论"的神灵观念和信仰逻辑中，各个宗教才能在今天的全球时代焕发出新一轮的生机，不同宗教之间也才会应天顺势、与时俱进，化历史为神奇、化干戈为玉帛，相互补益、共度人类。因此，这种"宇宙－精神论"，就是我们从中部文明的众多宗教中、特别是从"上帝至高无上"和"真主只有一个"的犹太教－基督教－伊斯兰教成果中，提炼出来的全新的神灵观念和信仰逻辑。

众神共一，就其普泛性而言，就是神神共一；就其深刻性而言，就是神性共一。

我们认为，这种揭示了众神共一的"宇宙－精神论"的神性学说、信仰理念，立足宇宙本质的宗教原则，就是中部文明为全球文明提供的神灵观念和信仰逻辑。

三、结 论

以上论述说明什么呢？

它说明：人类生存形态从持续了几千年的"部落世界"、"国家世界"，经由最近三百年、特别是20世纪的"国家间世界"，正在迅速转入"全球世界"，处于这样一个时代，只有确立一种全球文明，才能从根本上改变人类的命运。

它说明：人类千百年来所讲的合一、和平、和谐、和合等，都是从事物外部、从人们的主观愿望出发的，具有外部"粘合"、人为"撮合"的特征；而"共一"则是从事物的内在本质出发的，是从事物的本性中发掘出共性、用共性反过来解释和提升个性的全新的认识方式。

它说明：正是西方文明中的万物共一精神、东方文明中的人类共一精神、中部文明中的众神共一精神，整合成了21世纪乃至未来更远时代的"全球文明精神"。

它说明：我们人类在完成了"猴子变人"那次学业之后，又开始了较之前次更加伟大的第二次学习期，这次学习的基本课程就是"全球文明"，就是"用文明的方式推进文明"。

是呵，万物共一、人类共一、众神共一，天下一家、天人合一、全球文明，这些思想早在两千多年前的老子、索罗亚斯德、"以赛亚"第二、苏格拉底、毕达哥拉斯、孔子、柏拉图、释迦牟尼、耶稣和稍后的穆罕默德等先哲那里，就被这样那样提出来了。不过，在那样的时代，这些思想只能是理想，只能是个别智者、圣者、觉者的超凡推测、天才憧憬。尽管他们倾其毕生去实施，其结果都因不合时宜而不了了之了。

与之不同，我们的时代，已经不再是原来那种彼此封闭、交往狭窄，农牧为本、目标短近，智力粗浅、人性混沌的时代。今天的时代，已经是人类飞速一体化、信息化的时代，是对微观世界的认识相当深入、对宏观世界的认知极为广阔的时代，是"全球社会"已经到来的时代，是"全球文明"抽芽吐翠的时代，是"世界历史"真正开始的时代，是"成熟人类"就要降生的时代，这就为实践三个共一的伟大事

81

业，提供了坚实的时代基础、足够的客观前提和适宜的知识背景。

古往今来，人人都在追求真、善、美，万物共一就是21世纪的"真"，人类共一就是21世纪的"善"，众神共一就是21世纪的"美"。

东方西方，人人都在向往知、情、意，万物共一就是全球时代的"知"，人类共一就是全球时代的"情"，众神共一就是全球时代的"意"。

古往今来，人人都在寻找地利、人和、天时，立足万物共一就会产生"地利"，倡导人类共一就会实现"人和"，走向众神共一就会迎来"天时"。

东方西方，人人都在呼唤自由、平等、博爱，立足万物共一才会有真正的"自由"，倡导人类共一才会有真正的"平等"，走向众神共一才会有真正的"博爱"。

立足万物共一——万物共有同一种决定－反决定本性，因而必定一体共通。

倡导人类共一——人人共具同一种自然－人道本性，因而必须互补共生。

走向众神共一——众神共秉同一种宇宙－精神本性，因而应当相生共荣。²⁴

---

24 如果把问题再进一步，万物、人类、神灵三者之间也是共一的。这种共一包括三个方面：一是因为万物、人类、神灵具有共一性，宇宙才能成为一个有机整体；二是因为人的肉体、人格、灵魂具有共一性，方才构成了人类生命体；三是宇宙有机体与人类生命体具有共一性，方才构成了东方人所说的天－地－人"三才体系"，才有了千百年来人们所说的"天人感应"，也才有了层出不穷的先知群体。所以，万物－人类－神灵，物性－人性－神性，也是共一的关系。

我们可以把这个问题再深入一层。

如果(像前面所说(决定反决定是宇宙的生成原因、建构原则、演进趋向，那么决定反决定就是宇宙精神中最根本的部分、是宇宙的灵魂；如果决定反决定是宇宙最根本的精神、是宇宙的灵魂，那么决定反决定就是一种精神性的实在、并且是终极性的精神实在。宇宙精神是创造了物理反映、植物感应、动物意识、人类理性的精神，所以，要理解这种终极性的精神，必须突破已成人类常识和共识的关于"动物意识"、"人类精神"等概念的思维定势和基本定义。

如果决定反决定是宇宙的终极精神实在，那么它就不仅具有各种"非终极精神"所以为精神的由低到高的五级属性：(1)映知性(如物理－化学反映)，(2)感知性(如这，就是本宣言的基本结论。

生物—植物感应)，(3)认知性(如许多动物的意识力、识别力)，(4)自知性(如人类的自我意识能力、反思能力)，(5)预知性(如先知们的先知先觉、特能人的遥感预见)，而且具有作为宇宙的终极精神所特有的由浅到深的五级属性：(1)直知性(无逻辑性)，(2)超知性(无证明性)，(3)原知性(无对象性)，(4)永知性(无历时性)，(5)全知性(无制约性)。

是的，在"前宇宙"期，众多前宇宙元素或"初始物能"通过前宇宙场或"原始场能"相对无序地相互作用着。这种相互作用的整体效果在逐渐"接近"——毋宁说在"寻找"一种结构，最后它们选择并确立了"决定—反决定结构"。因为，只有决定—反决定这种性质的相互作用才能克服前宇宙的无序性、对称性、可逆性，走向有序性、非对称性、不可逆性，实现稳定性、时间性、发展性。所以，决定反决定模式的确立，标志着这些纵横交织的决定反决定作用到达了由它所设定的那个确定的奇点、确定的临界。更为重要的是，这个奇点、这种临界的形成，意味着一种具有精神性质的新型能量——一种具有自反映、自调节、自创造、自超越性质的能量——灵能被创生出来。给初始宇宙和后来的宇宙以精神的解释，是宇宙学中一个最根本的问题。因为，只有这种"灵性"的能量才具有确立自身结构、选择运动目标并为实现目标而调整自身的能力。

这样，一个以灵能为主导、以决定反决定为本质、由物能—场能—灵能整合而成的开元性的能量体系诞生了，它就是宇宙；使物能、场能、灵能整合成一个自构成、自进化的整体的力量即是宇宙的精神；而催生出宇宙精神并体现其自构成、自演进这一实质的东西，便是决定反决定。所以，把万事万物置于"网络关系"之中从而使它们变成了、并强化着一个个"能量性介体"，把宇宙变成"能量体系"从而使它获得了、并提高着灵性和知性，把物能、场能、灵能结合为"有机整体"从而使宇宙具有了、并增强着确定秩序和演进方向，以及将这种秩序规则和演进矢向贯彻到宇宙的各个层次之中、操纵于各个层次之间，这是决定反决定的真正奥妙，也是它的伟大意义。当然也可以说，这就是上帝的奥秘和意义。奥地利著名科学家埃里克·詹奇曾经说："上帝不是造物主，而是宇宙的意识"。其实，道理应当是这样的："上帝就是造物主，因为它是宇宙的意识。"

是这样的，由于以决定反决定为实质的宇宙精神具有映知性、感知性、认知性、自知性、预知性，特别是具有独特的直知性、超知性、原知性、永知性、全知性，所以它才能呈现出以决定反决定为根本性质的宇宙模式，维持着以决定反决定为基本规则的宇宙秩序，遵循着由"决定—反决定效应"所预设的宇宙过程；而我们人类、我们这个具有自然—人道性质的地球人类生命群体，则是宇宙经过漫长的孕育，到了"必须产生"时才应运而生的一种全新的宇宙形态。所以，宇宙—精神论是"关于宇宙本质的理论"，决定—反决定论是"关于宇宙精神的本质的理论"，而自然—人道论则是"关于宇宙精神如何创生了地球人类、赋于人类以自然—人道本性、并让人类因这种本性而确立起'人性—类性'这一生存方式的理论"。或者简单地说，宇宙因选择了决定反决定而具有了精神，人类因宇宙精神而具有了自然—人道本性，决定反决定则通过宇宙—精神、自然—人道而成了自己。可见，决定—反决定，自然—人道，宇宙—精神，这三者之间有着内在的共一性。

如果三个共一也是共一的关系，那么：(1)宇宙的产生，不过是"前宇宙"的决定性成份与其反决定成份经过极其漫长的相互吸引和精心调试，最终耦合而成的"奇点效应"(比如，耗散结构理论所说的发散点，生命科学所讲的物种分化点，人类的意识和良知的发生点，都源于这种"奇点效应")；(2)宇宙的秩序，不过是宇宙的决定作用与反决定作用彼此渗透、相互支撑，从而使宇宙向外向内、向前向后都恰到好处即具有多重限定的"临界状态"(比如植物的"年轮"，动物的"寿命"等，都源于这种"临界状态")；(3)宇宙的过程，不过是宇宙在逐步实现由决定反决定精神制定的"过程预设"(比如生命形式的由低到高，个人的不同人生运程，人类认识事物之感性－知性－理性－悟性的顺序，等等，都源自这种"过程预设")；(4)宇宙的结局，不过是宇宙因内在的决定反决定作用而不断提升结构级别、不断生发新的素质、不断接近终极目标，却又永远不会突破决定反决定所规定的临界的序动过程；(5)人类的产生，不过是宇宙按照宇宙精神的要求，在演进"到了必须采用肉体－智力生命的自创造力量才能进入更高层次的演化时"的应时之物，因而人类生活的真正意义并不是像千万年来所做的那样，只为着自己忙碌、热衷于窝里打斗、到处去称王称霸，而是为宇宙的演进注入"生物性智力"的新素。

由此可见，导致了万物共一的决定－反决定，导致了人类共一的自然－人道，导致了众神共一的宇宙－精神，这三个共一之间也是共一的关系。如果借用《圣经》中的道理作比喻，决定－反决定就是宇宙的"圣灵"，宇宙－精神就是宇宙的"圣父"，自然－人道则是宇宙的"圣子"，而三者之间，也是《圣经》中所说的"三位一体"的关系。这里的三位一体，也还是三者共一。这里的三者共一所言又是决定反决定："决定－反决定"决定着"宇宙－精神"，"宇宙－精神"决定着"自然－人道"，后者依次地反决定于前者。

由于本宣言的主要任务是从理论上解决人类自身的文明问题，因而对人类的意义、宇宙的精神、神灵的本质，以及三者之间的共一性，均未作详尽的阐述。

Appendix One

An Open Letter to UN a discussion on the establishment of a World United Government

Passed and adopted in The Second World Congress of Global Civilization

 The Organization for Promoting Global Civilization

www.opgc.net
November 14-16, 2005, UN Millennium Plaza, New York

AN OPEN LETTER SENT BY The Second World Congress of Global Civilization Proposing to the United Nations General Assembly A Discussion on the Establishment of a World United Government

(1) The Secretariat of the Second World Congress of Global Civilization, herewith submits this open letter[1] to the United Nations General Assembly proposing a discussion on the establishment of a World United Government.

The complete structure and administration of the proposed government has been set forth by Professor Shaohua Zhang in his book, *My Ideals of a World United Government*. Professor Zhang is the Chairman of the Organization for Promoting Global Civilization (OPGC), the organization sponsoring the Second World Congress of Global Civilization at the United Nations Plaza in New York from November 14-16, 2005.

(2) The First World Congress of Global Civilization was held from July 16-18, 2001 in Sydney, Australia. The Congress adopted a resolution promoting the spirit of "Global Civilization" encompassing religious, cultural and political cooperation. In the Declaration of Global Civilization, the Congress tried to create what was described as "a guidepost for mankind at the crossroads of an era of globalization." After the September 11th terrorist attack against the United States, Professor Zhang proposed to the international community that the day should be officially remembered as "Global Civilization Day" to emphasize the urgent need for world peace in a world still dominated by political, religious and cultural conflicts. However, the alarm was not heard. Soon after the attack, the United States and Britain led the war against the Taliban in Afghanistan and then against Iraq. After the Iraq war was officially declared over, a series of attacks erupted in Russia, Saudi Arabia, Israel, Palestine, India, Pakistan, Morocco and Indonesia. These attacks were aimed at local and foreign governments, political leaders, military forces, and even religious targets. The people of the world are concerned that these attacks will become more frequent, indiscriminate, and destructive, causing more international turmoil.

In the first years of this new century, such sinister developments in the international political arena are a stark reminder of the violent conflicts of the last century. Humankind is on the verge of repeating this tragic history. The Second World Congress of Global Civilization proposes this open letter before the United Nations General Assembly in an attempt to encourage a break with humanity's pernicious past. It is hoped that this new idea for cooperation in world governance will serve as a guideline for our future international political development.

1　This open letter was drafted by Shaohua Zhang. Chinese version is the standard version. This English version was translated by OPGC translation team.

(3) In light of our multi-polar world and ever increasing global integration, people of the world should rethink the meaning of such traditional terms as "nation," "race," "religion" and "culture." How will people in the global village balance the traditional idea of national sovereignty and the reality of globalization? How will they balance the interests of a single nation against the welfare of all human beings? The United Nations Secretary General, Kofi Annan, stated the dilemma in his Millennium Report, "Simply put, our post-war institutions were built for an inter-national world, but we now live in a global world. Responding effectively to this shift is the core institutional challenge for world leaders today."

The most pressing issue for humankind is to have the fortitude to embrace the emergence of this "global world." We can work towards this spirit of "Global Civilization" only through a governing entity, which can objectively look at the world's problems. OPGC has set forth in this open letter a proposal for just such an entity. Motivated by the ideals set forth in this open letter, OPGC has decided to feature the topic of "World United Government" at the top of its agenda for its upcoming Second World Congress.

(4) Concepts such as a world government have a distinguished history. After the end of World War II, this idea was formulated by a group of world-renowned scientists and scholars, such as, Albert Einstein, and the celebrated historian, Arnold Toynbee. Their inspiration grew out of concern over the atomic bombing of Japan and its dark portent for the future. Their motives were to safeguard world peace by putting nuclear weapons under strict international control and to remedy the drawbacks intrinsic to the system of the United Nations, so it could better cope with the world's problems.

In his political essay, "Towards a World Government," Albert Einstein noted, "A world government must be created which is able to solve conflicts between nations by judicial decision. This government must be based on a clearcut constitution which is approved by the governments and nations and which give them sole disposition of offensive weapons." Furthermore, in his 1947 commentary on the United Nations, titled "An Open Letter to the General Assembly of the United Nations," Einstein stated, "As long as there is a conflict of authority between the Assembly and the Security Council, the effectiveness of the whole institution will remain necessarily impaired…The method of representation at the United Nations should be considerably modified. The present method of selection by government appointment does not leave any real freedom to the appointee. Furthermore, selection by governments cannot give the peoples of the world the feeling of being fairly and proportionately represented."

However, the prophetic insight of Einstein and his colleagues was lost on the international community due to the immense post war reconstruction effort that was a priority for most countries.

(5) In response to Secretary General Kofi Annan's repeated calls for "renewing the United Nations," OPGC has taken the initiative in appealing for the establishment of a World United Government that will differ from the United Nations both in its nature and in its organization. In the OPGC proposal, the United Nations will continue to exist, emerging as the World United Parliament, exercising legislative power while the prospective World United Government will be the highest executive body.

Aspiring to prevent further devastating wars from occurring, Franklin Roosevelt, Winston Churchill, Joseph Stalin, Chiang Kei-sheik, and other leaders worked together to create the United Nations sixty years ago. They were strategically farsighted, politically sagacious, profoundly humane, and unusually tactful in establishing an international organization that has been performing great works in the six decades since its foundation.

However, the last sixty years have proven the problematic aspects of the United Nations as pointed out by Einstein. Even at its best, the United Nations has been acting merely as an international forum or contenting itself with playing the role of a mediator. This stems from the fact that the United Nations has never been granted supreme political or military authority, nor entitled to generate independent revenue. It also lacks a series of ordinances supported by all national governments, including ordinances to regulate the conduct of member states, leaders of nations, political parties and military forces. Since the United Nations is not a sovereign entity, nor a real federation of states, it cannot act as a supranational entity even though it has been called on to resolve global issues such as ethnic, state and religious conflicts, government oppression and sustainable use of natural resources. International politics continue to be dominated by the imbalance of power that exists between large and small countries, and between powerful and weak nations. "The strong do what they have the power to do and the weak accept what they have to accept," is still as true today as it was 2,500 years ago when Thucydides wrote it.

Contrary to the current United Nations, the World United Government would be vested with the full spectrum of authority and power that duly belongs to a supranational government. Moreover, it would be structurally different from any other federation that has ever existed.

In recent centuries, the world witnessed the emergence of three categories of political federation. The first category is a federal system characterized by an assembly of individual states, such as the United States and the Russian Federation where the central government operated as the highest authority. The second category was characterized by a bloc of nations that united with the goal of becoming more prosperous as a group while remaining individual sovereignties, such as the European Union. The third category of federation provides a meeting platform where nation-states are able to work together on issues and resolve differences peacefully, such as the United Nations.

However, all three types of government have limitations. The United States has incurred difficulties in resolving disputes between state and federal authority. The European Union went through decades of internal strife before it officially emerged. Nevertheless the member states believed that entering such a federation was beneficial and thus sought to be included. As for the United Nations, many member states simply treat it as a "rubber stamp."

There are two explanations for the different outcomes of these three forms of federation. The success of a federation is directly dependent on, first the manner in which nations within the federation are allied with each other, and second the long-term goals and purposes of the federation beyond the initial utilitarian reason for its founding.

Upon their inception, each of the three categories of federation specified above were simply means for coping with immediate needs. The majority of these federations were *ad hoc* at the beginning and were markedly deficient in the soundness of their philosophical groundwork. While they served the purposes they were initially designed for, they had various degrees of political underdevelopment to be considered a "supranational entities" as demonstrated by their severe organizational difficulties.

The structure of the World United Government conceptualized by OPGC is different, since it incorporates the best of all three federations. World United Government will be endowed with the centralized power to exercise political authority over all state governments. It will guarantee political independence to all state governments in the world in the same way as the European Union. Finally, it will provide the platform to promote cooperative political interaction between state governments that is unique to the United Nations. The relationship between the World United Government and the state governments under its jurisdiction will be both hierarchical and mutually supervisory. Under normal circumstances they will interact on a consultative basis. In emergencies however, the state governments will be obligated to comply with the World United's political authority.

(6) Theory analysis tells us we are human because, as Aristotle asserts, we are political animals. This political nature has caused the development of nationalism and ethnocentrism, and thus we have a sense of responsibility to do whatever it takes for the sake of our nation. We have a sense of honor propelling us to do both good and evil in the name of patriotism. We hold a sense of gratitude in our right hand and a sense of hatred in the left. We have a way of organizing ourselves so that we seek similarity, while attacking what is different. We have the courage to be a hero as well as a killer. We have the knowledge to make machines; machines that improve lives in the morning and machine guns that destroy lives in the afternoon—for the sake of our nation and state.

In addition, traditional ideas such as "nationalism," "religious zeal," and "cultural acceptance" that are held in high esteem contribute to this duality. In this rapidly changing world, these conventional concepts are the origin of many conflicts.

The proposed World United Government promotes global thinking instead of nationalism, and offers all people the opportunity to come together as one human family. Only under the rubric of such a global government will nations and leaders be motivated to work towards global harmony instead of national interests. Only then will nations and political parties be transformed into key entities with the means for promoting global welfare, improving the environment and achieving world peace.

(7) Today we are faced with a reality that is dominated by globalization and characterized by highly technological advancements in every aspect of life. It is also a time of increasing military mobilization by governments, and increasing developments in powerful weaponry. In a world ruled by the power of the gun, filled with historical prejudice and hatred and where countries covet other countries' resources, no one nation is really safe and no defense system is ultimately effective. It is inevitable that in such a world, no government would conduct itself altruistically and no individual would work unselfishly.

(8) History has proven that whenever people organize into a larger political entity, from a tribe to a nation-state and then to a federation, the political reorganization helps to prevent internecine wars and acts as a catalyst towards greater unity. History is now pushing us into a global village where there is no one religion, country or federation that is capable of single-handedly resolving wars, ethnic tensions, preventing terrorism, dissemination of nihilistic hatred or eliminating the sources of inequality among nations and people. In such a time in history, we believe that the establishment of a world government is the only alternative promising true peace and security for all nations, and cooperation amongst them.

Only the World United Government proposal has the ability to guarantee that the prospective "World United Parliament," its prototype being the United Nations of today, be vested with the authority over the world that needs the assurance of peace and harmony for humanity. It is equally clear that only such a global structure has the ability to spare the world from disasters brought about by the short-sighted policies of governments, and unwarranted military aggression. Only such a global entity can possess the necessary means to ensure that the resources of weak countries are protected from the avarice of more powerful neighbors.

(9) History is the best teacher for humankind. History has been pointing towards one right direction but providing a myriad of wrong choices for humans so we can learn and grow from our mistakes and struggles. Whenever we have come to a precarious period in history and have not realized the gravity of the

situation, then destiny saved us from ourselves and directed us to the right path at the crucial moment. The trend of history has been a journey from tribal society to nation-state then to multi-national federations such as the European Union and the United Nations. The apex of humankind would be a final progression to a world government.

Political leaders should learn from history. During the era of tribal societies when people were isolated, the advancement of the society depended upon the wisdom of its leaders. Even during the era of nation-states when technology was still in its infancy, the advancement of the state relied on its heads of state. However, in the era of globalization and instant information where people can share knowledge from every corner of the earth, it is nearly impossible for any nation to remain in isolation anymore. Our leaders have yet to demonstrate the capability to adjust to the speed of this rapidly changing world. Today, the question of establishing an evolved system of world government is a test for the political wisdom of our leaders. It is a test for the real faith of religious leaders. It is also a test of ethical standards for scholars around the world. Whenever history comes to a point that calls upon the courage and responsibility of those leaders to decide our destiny, any hesitation is an excuse, any such excuse is a crime, any such crime will only harm the well-being of every global citizen. Similarly, any form of self-interest is an obstacle that could make humankind losing a great historical opportunity to step into a brighter future.

OPGC is proposing four principles that express the hope and desire for global citizens:

- Consider progressive ideas from all schools of thought
- Understand cultural differences from a holistic perspective of humanity
- Act in the interest of global well-being rather than for regional interests
- Resolve conflicts through common principles and sense of justice.

(10) It is the right time to engage in this vital discussion and present a serious proposal to the United Nations.

The time is right, because each of us can only have one life, yet the number of weapons of mass destruction on earth today can kill six billion people sixty times. The time is right when powerful nations display their might with new weapon systems year after year. The time is right when undeveloped countries endlessly fight civil wars while falling deeper into poverty. The time is right when countries ruled by dictators praise themselves on their democratic achievements. The time is right when on the one hand, many conflicts can be resolved with the creation of the European Union and the African Union, yet on the other hand, new global competitions with fresh conflicts are also created. The time is right, when science and technology lead us into the space, information, and clone age, yet global politics are dominated by outdated policies. In 1789, "The Declaration of Rights of Man" of the National Constituent Assembly in France quoted Confucius when it stated, "do not impose on others what you yourself would not want imposed upon you." But in today's global political landscape, this famous maxim has been changed to its antithesis, "impose onto others what you, yourself do not want imposed upon you." The time is right, for the well-being of humanity, for the hope of the world, for the birth of a new civilization, for the marching progress of history. The time is now, here, today, history is calling upon you to act with your vote.

(11) As this open letter draws to a close, we would like to pay homage once more to Franklin Roosevelt, the 32nd president of the United States and one of the founders of the United Nations. He tragically died two months before the adoption of the Charter of the United Nations, but on the last day of his life he wrote a message to guide us in our future endeavors when plagued with doubt, "The only obstacle to realizing the goals we set for tomorrow is the suspicion attached to today. So let us just march on firmly in aspiring confidence."

Thank you.

Delegates of Second World Congress of Global Civilization
November 14-16, 2005

Appendix Two

The Original Version of The Open Letter in Chinese

全球文明第二届世界大会关于建议联大讨论"成立世界联合政府"的公开信

（全球文明第二届世界大会通过）

尊敬的主席先生，各国代表，各位朋友：

(1)受全球文明第二届世界大会委托，全球文明第二届世界大会秘书处特向联大提交这封"建议联大讨论'成立世界联合政府'的公开信"。

世界联合政府的建构原则、完整框架和运作模式，由全球文明推进组织(OPGC)主席和全球文明第一届、第二届世界大会主席章韶华在他的《世界联合政府构想》一书中提出。

(2)2001年7月16—18日，全球文明第一届世界大会在澳大利亚悉尼希尔顿饭店召开，会议决定在世界范围内推进"全球文明精神"，通过了被一些与会者称作"为全球时代的人类指明了前进道路"的《全球文明宣言》。

会后53天，9.11事件爆发，证明了此次大会的预见性和重要性；第二天即9月12日，章韶华代表OPGC向全世界发出倡议，在全球世界、信息时代，一国一地一人如果仍旧坚持政治对抗、宗教对立、文化对撞，都会迅即波及世界、殃及全球，因而建议联合国大会同意将每年的"9.11"定为"全球文明日"。然而，这个声音仍没有引起人们的重视，25天后，美英等国打响了阿富汗战争；又17个月，美英等国绕开联合国发动了伊拉克战争；战争结束之后，俄罗斯、沙特阿拉伯、以色列、巴勒斯坦、印度、巴基斯坦、摩罗哥、印度尼西亚……发生了一系列报复性爆炸事件。在这些事件中，有的是针对别国或本国的政府和领导人，有的是针对对方的军事威胁和宗教信仰，有的是针对似乎永远挥之不去的历史上的是是非非、恩恩怨怨。而更加让人担忧的是，类似的恶性国际政治事件，不仅会毫无疑问的越发严重，而且会毫无疑问的更加无序。

国际政治发展的严峻局面证明了OPGC1999年的预言：新千年的开始正在重现旧千年开始时的许多特征，新世纪初的人类正在拉开上个世纪初的悲剧序幕。为了防止人类严重局势的升级，全球文明第二届世界大会筹委会决定，正式向联大提交这封公开信。

(3)仔细分析新世纪发生的几场战争和所有恐怖事件，真正的原因只有一个，这就是人类如何在政治上应对"生存的全球性"。面对今天这个以"多极对立世界"为表象的"全球一体世界"，人类应该怎么做，是顺应全球时代的到来，勇敢地走进全球、面对时代、开创未来，还是像今天绝大数国家所做的那样，返回传统、回到民族、回归本土，或者仍然坚持对抗、争夺霸权、崇尚武力？换言之，生活在"全球世界"中的我们，应当如何处理传统理念与现代生活、国家情结与全球时代、民族追求与人类利益的关系。亦如联合国秘书长安南在《我们的民众：秘书长千年报告》中所说：包括联合国在内许多战后的国际机构，"是前辈们为了一个国家间世界建造的，但我们目前生活在一个全球世界中。有效地应付这一转变是今天世界各国领导人在体制上面对的核心挑战。"(第30节)进一步讲，各国领导人终归是自己的国家、民众、党派的忠实代表，所以，根本说来，这是全人类共同面对的一场世界政治体制上的核心挑战。

其实，早在1999年OPGC成立不久，即以信件的方式向联合国、各国政府、各大宗教同时发出呼吁：在即将到来的新世纪新千年，最重要的问题是有没有承认"全球世界正在形成"这一事实的勇气，最大的难题是获得正确处理旧的生存方式与新的时代生活的智慧，最紧迫的工作是适时地确立一种"全球文明精神"、成立一个"世界联合政府"（包括成立世界联合政府的直属机构，如：人类前景规划组织，地球生态保护组织，世界和平保卫组织，公民权利保障组织，全球经济协作组织，世界宗教联合组织，全球文明推进组织，等等）。正是基于这种认识，OPGC才把全球文明第一届世界大会的主题确定为讨论并通过《全球文明宣言》，将那次会议的会址选在以"倡导多元文化并存"著称的澳大利亚；基于同样的认识，又把此次大会的主题确定为"建议联合国大会讨论成立世界联合政府"，并将会址定在联合国所在地——美国纽约。

（4）成立世界联合政府，是20世纪伟大的理论物理学家阿尔伯特·爱因斯坦、著名的历史学家阿诺德·汤因比为代表的一些著名的科学家和学者，在二战结束不久、尤其是美国在日本使用了原子弹之后，为了严格管理和控制核武器、弥补联合国在体制上的缺陷，而提出的一个对于世界和平有着深远意义的世界政治课题。

爱因斯坦在《迈向一个世界政府》一文中写道："技术以及战争工具的发展似乎已使我们这颗行星缩小了。经济上的相互联系促使各国之间远比过去更加休戚相关。现在拥有的破坏性武器使地球上不存在任何一块可以免于突然性的总毁灭的地方。逃脱这一命运的唯一希望在于通过超国家的方式来确保和平。必须创建一个能够通过司法仲裁解决国家间冲突的世界政府。这个政府必须建立在所有政府与国家都一致同意的含义明确的宪章基础上，并由该宪章赋予其对进攻性武器的唯一处置权。任何个人或国家只有自愿将军事力量交与这个国际权威机构，并放弃任何利用武力在国外攫取利益的企图，甚至包括达到这一目的的工具，才能被认为是爱好和平的。"对于联合国，他在《致联合国大会的公开信》中说："只要在联合国大会和安理国之间存在权力的冲突，那么，整个机构的有效性必将受到损害；现行的通过政府任命来选派代表的方法，并没有给被任命者以任何真正的自由，而且由政府选派代表的作法不能让世界各民族感觉到代表的产生是公正的，按比例进行的。"

　　但是，由于那时联合国刚刚成立，正处在兴旺时期，其自身的时代局限和体制弊病尚未显露出来，加之当时多数国家正由绵延不断的民族战争、特别是连续两次世界大战，转向劫后复苏、战后重建，因此，爱因斯坦等人的超前睿智未能引起人们的重视。

　　(5)我们建议成立的"世界联合政府"，既是爱因斯坦这一事业的继续，也是对联合国秘书长安南一再呼吁"革新联合国"的积极响应。具体地说，世界联合政府的建立与今日联合国的改革乃是同一个问题的两个方面：一方面，联合国经过改革和转型而成为世界各国公民共同的最高的立法机构——"世界联合国会"；另一方面，世界联合政府将成为世界上唯一的最高的行政机构。

　　60年前，为了从根本上防止两次世界大战这类灾难性事件的发生，罗斯福(美国)、丘吉尔(英国)、斯大林(前苏联)、蒋介石(中国)等人，以其高远的战略眼光、非凡的政治智慧、博大的人道情怀和高超的运作艺术，适时地创建了联合国。60年来，联合国为人类的进步和世界的和平，做出了令我们的子子孙孙永远不能忘怀的卓越贡献。

　　但是，到了60年后的今天，我们不仅越来越强烈地感受到了爱因斯坦当年发现的问题，而且还暴露出了一系列新的更加严重的问题。例如，由于联合国充其量不过是一个由各成员国任命的代表所组成的"世界议会"、"国际论坛"，就是说，由于它在几乎所有的世界重大事务中没有政治上的最高权力、军事上的最大威力、经费上的合理来源，没有各国必须严格遵守的统一的世界宪法体系、世界行政体系、世界道德体系，没有控制国际秩序正向运行的世界联合国会体系、世界众议体系、世界参议体系、世界政议体系，没有各国政府必须共同遵守的诸如国家法、政党法、国家元首法、国家军事法等一些约束各国战争行为、各国政党行为、各国元首对内对外行为、各国军备行为的世界法律体系，一句话，由于它既不是"联合"而成的"国"、也不是"国"的真正"联合"，既不具备超国家政府的性能、又要面对属于超国家政府才能够处理的问题，这就使得它在处理民族与民族、国家与国家、宗教与宗教、主权与类权、人权与政权、人类与环境等诸多关系时，常常力不从心，往往南辕北辙，多数情况下不得不停留于观察员、调解员和外交辞令。正是由于这一点，所以直到今天，大国无宽容，小国无主权，强国无良知，弱国无外交，仍然是国际政治运行的一条铁律。联合国对许多重大国际政治问题上的无奈、忧虑和尴尬，在座的诸位，感受是最深的，也是相似的。

与之不同，我们倡导成立的这种世界联合政府，正是克服联合国体制上的这些弱点和缺点的产物。

世界联合政府的根本特点是"联合"。从历史上看，人类曾经采用过三种国家之间的政治联合方式：第一种是把不同国家集中在一起的"集中式"联合，如美国、俄罗斯等；第二种是为保护不同国家主权更好发挥作用的"集合式"联合，如欧盟、非盟等；第三种是为了让不同国家能够聚在一起求同存异、并且主要在外交层面上的"集约式"联合，如联合国。第一种联合如美国，它先是险些毁于南北战争、今天又显现出了诸多世所共知的弊端；第二种联合如欧盟，它的形成酝酿了近30年，成立不久其内部便发生了一系列严重分歧；作为第三种联合的联合国，在其初期就阻力重重、在今天更是被许多国家当成了"橡皮图章"。这三种联合的命运之所以如此，是因为它们自始至终都隐含着两个深层问题：第一，进入欧盟体系的国家说"联合很好"，而各国对待联合国的态度是既想弃之不用，又在视之如命。可见，真正的问题不是要不要联合，而是国与国之间在政治上究竟为什么联合和应当怎么样联合，对此，上述三种联合模式都没有解决；第二，作为一种超国家性政治机构，上述三种联合的大多数(如欧盟)一开始就是基于单一目的，一开始就缺乏一种坚实的理论基础，特别是一开始就没有站在"世界整体"的高度、缺乏为了"全体人类"的胸襟。所以，这三种联合虽然有它们产生的理由，却也有着明显的单面性和作为超国家组织形式的不成熟性。

我们所说的世界联合政府不同于上述任何一种，而又整合了、提升了三种联合中的政治经验。就是说，世界联合政府既有联邦模式中的政治集中——在世界政治中具有最高的权威，又具有欧盟模式中各成员国的政治独立——国家之间彼此有着完全独立的主权，同时还具有联合国模式中的政治集约——世界联合政府与主权国家政府既有目标上的一致性、又有职权上的区别性，既是领导与被领导的关系、又是监督与被监督的关系，既在平常情况下采取政治协商、又在特殊情况下各国政府必须对世界联合政府以政治服从。

(6)从理论上讲，我们所以为"人"，正如古希腊哲学家亚里士多德所说，是因为我们人类是一个"政治性"的生命种群。由于这种生存本性，我们创造了部落、民族、国家。由于人类长期以来都是以部落、民族、国家的方式存在的，所以，我们有了责任感——一面报效祖国一面报复他国，我们有了荣誉感——既能做教人的圣人又能做杀人的英雄，我们有了情感——左手握着感恩右手攥着仇恨，我们有了组织——一方面"党同"一方面"伐异"，我们有了勇气——既可视死如归又能杀人如麻，我们有了知识——上午制造机器下午研制武器。

我们每个人之所以被一分为二为正相矛盾的"两性人"，除去人类进化阶段上的原因，更重要的，正好要归咎于千百年来约定俗成的、至今仍被人类视之如命的诸如国家意识、民族情结、教派偏执、文化自尊、党派习性。这些东西在民族中心时代、国家中心时代是无可厚非的，但在人类日益一体化的今天，它们则正好成了世界动荡和动乱的主要根源。这也就是说，只有当地球成了大家庭、人类成了一家人，国家、民族、宗教、政党才有可能摆脱劣根性弊端，转而成为促进世界大同、实现人人平等、维护天下太平、改善地球生态的最重要的机构和最有力的手段，60亿人的人性也才从此有了得以改善和提升的政治环境。问题在于，只有当全人类都在同一个世界联合政府的领导下，人类才能真正成为一家。如此说来，成立世界联合政府，就不仅仅是国家政体、国际政治发展到今天的要求，更是适应人类进化期以转变国家职能、提升民族精神、实现人性飞跃的需要。

(7)从现实上讲，我们正处于生存全球化、交往信息化、工具智能化的时代，但它同时又是公民精神民族化、军事权力国有化、武器性能规模化、国际矛盾白热化的时代。

在这样一个只有用枪炮才能维持下去的世界里，在这样一个枪炮里装的全是历史上的是非恩怨、现实中的偏见成见的世界里，在这样一个每个国家都永不满足因而眼睛紧盯着别国资源和财富的世界里，没有一个国家、一个人是安全的，也没有一个国家、一个人的积极防御是最终有效的，当然也不可能有一个国家的运作、一个人的行为能够真正朝向真理和良知。

(8)从历史上看，"民族"的形成基本上结束了氏族之间长达数万年的持续争战，"国家"的诞生基本上结束了民族之间长达数千年的世代仇杀，欧盟、非盟、阿盟的成立也基本上结束了长达数百年的区域内混战，那么，在人类进入"地球村"时代的今天，在没有任何一种宗教可以用"本教的完美"来说服和同化其它任何一种宗教的今天，在没有任何一个国家能够真正解决另外任何一个国家的任何一个问题的今天，在没有任何一个大国能够化解文明冲突、国际战争、民族对立的今天，在没有任何一个富国能够消除人类的不平衡根源、不平等根源、不公正根源的今天，在没有任何一个国际联盟能够制止仇恨蔓延、邪恶蔓延、恐怖蔓延的今天，成立世界联合政府便成了唯一一条世界和平之路、人类希望之路、国家安全之路。

例如，只有世界联合政府，才能真正确立日后的"世界联合国会"——今日联合国以至高无上的权威；又如，只有世界联合政府，才能最终消除因少数国家的政治理念、少数国家的首脑品格、少数国家的军事扩张、少数国家的历史复仇，给别国、给世界带来的麻烦和灾难；再如，只有世界联合政府，才能真正保证富裕国家用自己优越的民主政治制度、世代的辛勤劳动换来的财富不被别国别人平分和哄抢，才能真正保证弱小国家的各种资源不被别国别人瓜分和侵吞。

(9)历史规律是人类最好的导师。在人类前进的每一个历史时期，它都给人类提供一种正确选择、多种错误选择，以便让人类在自己的错误中寻找正确、在痛苦的磨练中得到提升。但是，当着人类在错误道路上或不知所措或不思悔改的时候，它便力挽狂澜，瞬间把人类带出绝境、送上正途。从部落酋长制度经民族自治制度到国家政府制度，从国家政府制度经联合国制度到世界联合政府制度，这是人类政治体制和人类自我管理方式发展的规律所使然。

历史规律也是个人、特别是领袖个人最好的导师。在彼此封闭、科技蒙昧、进步缓慢的民族中心时代、国家中心时代，民族的进步、国家的变革总是依赖于某个人、特别是领袖个人的变化。但在生存全球化、交往信息化、工具智能化、思维共振、成果共享、不同领域因彼此催化而日新月异的今天，世界的发展、人类的进步要比个人的变化快得多。这也就是说，在今天，是否同意成立世界联合政府，已经成了衡量今天各国政治领袖政治智慧高低的试金石，成了衡量今天各个宗教领袖宗教信仰真伪的分水岭，成了衡量今天各国学界领袖治学道德好坏的参照系。因为，在人类历史按照自身规律，需要领袖们勇敢地站出来担起历史责任的时候，任何反对的理由都是借口，任何一种借口都是在犯罪，任何一种犯罪都将殃及全人类的福祉；同样，与全人类的福祉相比，任何个人的既得利益都是蝇头小利，任何蝇头小利都会幻变成巨大障碍，任何一种障碍都有可能使自己丧失人生飞跃的历史良机、都有可能使人类的正当前进遭受挫折。

"用现代智慧扬弃传统理念，用人性大同解析民族小异，用全球公义把握区域利益，用文明共性化解文化冲突。"应当说，OPGC的这个宗旨，准确地表达了生活在"全球世界"中的绝大多数人们的愿望。

(10)是时候了，我们人类该是将"成立世界联合政府"的问题提请联合国大会严肃讨论、郑重表决的时候了。

是时候了，我们每个人的生命只有一次，但我们手中的各种武器特别是大规模杀伤性武器却足以让60亿人每人死上60次。是时候了，我们的军事强国多年来只能令人发笑地靠国家防御系统的升级来展示自己的强大。是时候了，我们那些本来贫弱的国家却在用取之不尽的方式、用之不竭的精力制造各种内乱和进一步的赤贫。是时候了，我们那些专制独裁的国家反而能用全民公决、全票通过的方法捍卫独裁、讴歌专制。是时候了，欧盟、非盟、阿盟等区域性国际联盟的成立，一方面解决了地域圈内、文明圈内的众多历史难题，但在另一方面，却预示着人类将从"国家间冲突"升级为"区域间冲突"———也就是真正意义上的"世界冲突"。是时候了，我们的智慧已经在科技领域发展到太空时代、信息时代、克隆时代，但在国际关系领域仍旧奉行着胜者为王、败者为寇的"王寇规则"，弱肉强食的"动物法则"，有奶就是娘的"婴儿思维"，宁可我负天下人、不可天下人负我的"疯子逻辑"。是时候了，法国《人权宣言》引用的中国圣人孔子的"已所不欲，勿施于人"这句话，正被今天的人们涂改成"己所不欲，才施于人"。是时候了，我们的总统、国王、君主没有一个敢为自己的子女承诺"你们是安全的"，更何况他的悠悠臣民！

是时候了，人类的福祉，世界的希望，文明的新生，历史的跃迁，就在今天，就在今天我们开会的这个大厅，就在你们今天的"举手之劳"。

(11)这封公开信就要结束了，我们又一次想到了联合国的主要缔造者、美国第32-35任总统富兰克林·罗斯福，他在《联合国宪章》通过之前的二个多月不幸去逝，临终的那一天，他这样写道："实现明天目标的唯一阻碍就是今天的疑虑，让我们怀着坚定而积极的信心奋勇前进吧！"

全球文明第二届世界大会代表(代表签字附后)
2005年11月14—16日

Appendix Three

About OPGC and five Congresses of Global Civilization

The Organization for Promoting Global Civilization (OPGC) is an international non-for-profit, non-governmental, academic organization. It was initiated by Chinese scholar Shaohua Zhang in 1998 and founded in October 1999 in Sydney, Australia by a group of scholars from the United States, Russia, China, the United Kingdom, Iran, Romania, India, Singapore, Australia, New Zealand, Canada, and Malaysia. In the first board meeting, held from December 2 to December 9, 1999, Shaohua Zhang was elected as Chairman; Professors Norman Levine from the United States, Titarenko from Russia, David McLellan from the United Kingdom, and Moshen Mohebbi from Iran, as well as Master Khooh Yong Tan from Singapore were elected as Vice-Chairs.

In 2005, OPGC moved the headquarters to New York City where the United Nations and many multinational organizations are located. It is a 501(C)(3) organization approved by the IRS (Internal Revenue Service, the USA).

OPGC believes that cultural conflicts and civilization clashes are increasingly intensified in the global world. Humanity is now in the most critical turning point in history and faces two choices—either going toward world peace and unity or going toward destruction. In order to avoid future tragedies and guide humanity into a better future, mankind must rethink how it manages human society in terms of politics, spirituality, environment, and culture in the twenty-first century. The Global Civilization concept theorized by OPGC integrates the essences of Western, Eastern, and Middle Civilizations and elevates them into a universal civilization for all humans. Global Civilization has the following four principles:

- The Oneness of all Matter
- The Oneness of All Humans
- The Oneness of All Faiths
- All is One in the Universe

Guided by the concept of Global Civilization, OPGC is committed to providing practical solutions to make every aspect of human activity full of civilized humanity, to resolving conflicts between cultures, nations, and religions, and to achieving world peace, unity, and religious harmony.

One of the most important strategies of OPGC is to organize five global Congresses to address, discuss and raise public awareness of a necessary paradigm shift in five important subjects respectively. The first two Congresses have already occurred. All five congresses, in sequence, are:

1st Congress: Held in Sydney, Australia in 2001.Subject: Theory

2nd Congress: Held in New York, USA, in 2005. Subject: Politics

3rd Congress: to be held in Jerusalem in 2009. Subject: Spirituality

4th Congress: to be held in Moscow, Russia in 2013. Subject: Environment

5th Congress: to be held in Africa in 2017. Subject: Culture

The First World Congress was held in Sydney, Australia in 2001. Representatives from 37 countries attended this conference. *The Declaration of Global Civilization* was discussed, debated, and adopted during the Congress as the guiding principle of the OPGC.

The Second Word Congress was held in 2005. Representative from 38 countries were in attendance. *An Open Letter to UN General Assembly proposing a discussing of the establishment of a World United Government* was discussed and adopted in this conference.

OPGC is currently preparing for the 3rd Congress of Global Civilization which will be held in May 2009 in Jerusalem. *A proposal to improve spiritual understanding and achieve religious harmony in the global world* is to be discussed and seek to be adopted in this Congress.

The 4th World Congress of Global Civilization to be held in Moscow in 2013 with a theme of The Oneness of All Matter and a task to discuss, debate, and pass *The 50 years' planning for global management of a sustainable ecosystem* to be drafted and written by renowned scientists around the world.

The 5th World Congress of Global Civilization is to be held in 2017 in Africa. One of the tasks in this conference is to compile a textbook based on The Declaration of Global Civilization, to organize a group of educators and public speakers comprising influential politicians, religious scholars, and scientists from all over the world, to raise public awareness and understanding about the spirit of global civilization through activities targeted universities of every state and major media of the world.

About the translator

Vincent Law is from Australia. He holds an MBA with distinction from The University of Waikato, New Zealand and a Bachelor of Engineering degree from Dong Hua University, China. He is currently the Vice-Chair and Executive Director of OPGC and living in New York.

978-0-595-41264-8
0-595-41264-5